Projects

A Guide to Their Use and Design

Ernest J. Ingram

Detselig Enterprises Limited
Calgary, Alberta

Ernest J. Ingram

The University of Alberta

Canadian Cataloguing in Publication Data

Ingram, Ernest J., 1926-
Projects

Bibliography: p.
Includes index.
ISBN 0-920490-88-3
1. Educational evaluation. I. Title.
LB2822.75.I53 1989   379.1'54   C89-091202-5

© 1989 by Detselig Enterprises Limited
P.O. Box G 399
Calgary, Alberta T3A 2G3

Printed in Canada   SAN 115-0324   ISBN 0-920490-88-

Contents

iii

List of Figures

Foreword

This book presents an approach to problem solving in an educational setting – the project approach. It is a truism to say that educational organizations today are complex, and that the problems that inevitably arise in them are equally complex. Especially when performing such key functions as educational system and program assessment, policy analysis and development, program development, and evaluation, an educational administrator needs a method of solving problems which takes into account all relevant factors within and outside the organization.

The project approach is one such method, the one which I have found most useful over the past two decades while designing and directing projects for educational organizations at all levels from elementary to post-secondary. The method presented here has not only been used extensively in the field but has also been taught in the University of Alberta graduate program in educational administration. In developing and refining courses which incorporate the project approach to problem solving, my colleagues and I have found that there is no comprehensive book currently on the market which can be used as a guide for conducting educational projects. This book fills that need, incorporating concepts and practical techniques developed over many years of using and teaching the project approach to problem solving.

This book can be used by two groups of readers: (1) university educators who are preparing educational leaders to become effective problem solvers, and the students enrolled in these graduate preparation programs, and (2) those who are currently in positions of educational leadership and wish to design and conduct projects to solve specific problems.

With regard to the first group, the book is based on several beliefs about what is needed to prepare educational leaders. Successful educational leaders develop and use a broad knowledge base and a variety of conceptual, technical, and human skills to help them perform their roles. This knowledge base and set of skills are acquired throughout a person's career through a wide variety of modes – life experiences, general education,

ix

professional education, and experiences on the job.

There has been much debate about the role of formal education, general as well as professional, in developing this repertoire of knowledge and skills. Although most would agree that formal education should provide a wide variety of knowledge and experiences for learners, there is also general agreement that the major role of formal education is to provide opportunities for learners to develop the skills and concepts necessary to help them continue to learn as effectively and efficiently as possible. That is, the curriculum should emphasize the concepts and skills associated with the learning process itself. This is similar to the self-help concept held by all effective human service professionals. The old saying "If I give you a fish, I will have to give you another one tomorrow; if I teach you how to fish, you can continue to feed yourself," could be paraphrased in an educational setting: "If I teach you only one new method of teaching reading, I will have to teach you other new methods as they are developed; if I teach you how to inquire and how to solve problems related to the teaching of reading, you can keep yourself up to date." The concept of self-help in learning and problem solving applies equally well to the professional preparation of educational administrators as to the education of teachers, or the general education of K-12 students.

The most broadly applied set of concepts in the administration of educational systems has to do with administrative problem solving and the effective application of the skills necessary for this type of problem solving. One might therefore expect to find an emphasis on these concepts and skills in the curriculum and delivery modes used by schools of educational administration. Although this emphasis is not as prevalent as one might expect, it is slowly developing in many of the better schools.

This, then, is essentially a self-help book. The first group of readers, those involved in graduate preparation programs for educational administrators, can use it to understand the concepts and practise the skills required to conduct educational projects. The book takes the position that these concepts can be taught most effectively and the skills learned best through an integrated process including the development of a project proposal and the conduct of the project. The integration of the skills of data gathering and analysis into this process would also be desirable.

The second group of readers, those who are currently in educational leadership positions, can use the book as a practical guide to designing and conducting projects. The book incorporates several beliefs about the nature of educational leadership which are elaborated upon in the first chapter.

Acknowledgements

This book had its genesis in a course on project design developed by the author with the assistance of a number of colleagues. Over a period of several years, it developed from its original form – a loose collection of course outlines, lecture and discussion notes, assignments, and illustrations drawn from actual projects conducted by the author and his colleagues – to its present form. The assistance of numerous classes of graduate students in educational administration at the University of Alberta is acknowledged with thanks. Their use of, and reactions to, earlier drafts of the information and materials which make up this publication contributed greatly to its present content and form. I am especially grateful to my colleagues Gordon McIntosh, Craig Montgomerie, Frank Peters, and Ken Ward, who assisted in developing and teaching the course on project design and who also contributed materials and ideas for this publication. I would also like to express my sincere appreciation to Nancy Mattson, who edited the manuscript and prepared it for presentation to the publisher, and to Peggy Foster, who typed the manuscript and assisted with many other aspects of its preparation.

E.J.I.

Detselig Enterprises Ltd. appreciates the financial assistance for its 1989 publishing program from

Alberta Foundation for the Literary Arts
Canada Council
Department of Communications
Alberta Culture

1
The Nature
of Projects

This book has been prepared primarily for those who have been assigned, who assume, or who are preparing for leadership roles in education. Traditionally, leadership was viewed as those acts involving the influencing of others as well as the control of the situation and the context in such a way as to induce movement in the direction desired (Osborn, Morris, & Conner, 1984). Current views of leadership would accept these concepts but expand upon them. Bennis (1983), for example, has defined leadership as a process of translating a vision into reality and then sustaining it. Bennis and Nanus (1985) have elaborated on this definition by identifying specific phases of the leadership process – namely, the creation of a vision, communication of the vision to others, and institutionalization of the vision. Although, in education, these acts are generally associated with the line positions of trustee, superintendent, and principal, there are others who are often called upon (or who assume) responsibilities for leadership roles: teachers, central office staff, parents, committees, interest groups, and task forces. Therefore, leadership also includes the patterning of initiation, attention, activity, and reinforcement over time and involves a variety of people and positions entering, playing a role in, and then withdrawing from the process.

The effective performance of these leadership acts, especially the acts of translating vision into reality and sustaining or institutionalizing it, requires a substantial background of knowledge and considerable skill in (1) identifying key elements of the vision and related intentions which require institutionalization; (2) collecting and analyzing the data necessary to adequately inform the process of moving from intention to effective institutionalization; (3) identifying the issues influencing the decision making process; (4) generating alternative means of resolving the issues and

1

solving the problems; and (5) making decisions related to the process of moving from intention to action – the problem-solving process.

Although this problem-solving process can take many structural forms, a very effective form – the one which is the subject of this book – is the "project approach." Effective educational leaders make extensive use of the project approach to problem solving and are knowledgeable about and skilled in the design and management of projects. This chapter lays the groundwork for the rest of the book by defining the nature of projects.

Distinguishing Characteristics of Projects

To understand project design and management, one must first distinguish project activities from non-project activities and be able to judge when the project mode of operation is the most appropriate for the purposes of the activity being contemplated.

Various types of activities are associated with the operation of schools or school jurisdiction – for example, providing services to students and staff, administering the school and the system, developing programs, maintaining buildings and facilities, implementing new programs and practices, supervising instruction, evaluating programs and personnel, undertaking inservice education programs, teaching, and analyzing policy. Many of these activities can and probably should be carried out through a project mode.

Most of the following characteristics must be present if an activity or a set of activities is to be classified as a project.

A clearly stated and specific goal or set of goals. Although all activities have goals – that is, a desired result or destination – the goal statements in project types of activities are generally stated more clearly and more specifically than those of most non-projects. For example, the goal of providing student personnel services – a non-project activity – might be stated as "to provide students with the information and support services they require to move toward their educational objectives," whereas the goals stated for a project to evaluate a school scheduling program might be stated as "to examine and describe the objectives, activities, and outcomes of the Hopper Program as these have been developed and changed over time; and to consider possible alternative scheduling plans based on an examination of research and practice in scheduling, the experiences of the Hopper Plan, and the views and desires of the Board, the teaching staff, the students, and the parents."

A set of performance standards. An acceptable level of performance or a minimum level of product quality is often established for projects. These are not always stated in specific, substantive terms – for example, "students must obtain a minimum performance level of 75 on the HPLT" – though such performance expectations are not uncommon. Performance standards might also include statements such as "the product must be judged satisfactory by a panel of experts on the basis of previously established performance criteria," or "the data collecting instrument being developed must be tested for validity by acceptable tests approved by the Steering Committee for the Project."

Time constraints. All projects are constrained by some type of time limitation. This might be in terms of calendar time (time linked), the completion of some related activity (event linked), or both. Time constraints are generally stated in terms such as "the project is to be completed by July 1, 1988," or "the final report is to be presented no later than three weeks after the evaluation results have been released by the Department." In any case, a project has a definite life span.

A unique set of activities. A project constitutes a "once-through, nonrepetitive" set of activities. Although a similar project might be undertaken at a different time or in a different location, each project is unique – it has its own characteristics, life span, and end product.

A supplemental activity. A project is generally supplementary, an adjunct to the ongoing operations of the organization. Although a project is generally considered as something extra or as a special activity which is not part of the regular activities of the organization, this is not a necessary characteristic of projects conducted in educational organizations. Projects can and in some cases should become part of the mode through which educational organizations carry out their functions. Program development can be carried out through the project mode, as can the in-service functions, the evaluation functions, and even the teaching functions.

Specific budget constraints. The specific nature of project goals, the time constraints placed on projects, and the fact that they are generally considered supplementary activities contribute to the need to establish specific budgets, and in many cases tighter budget constraints and financial accounting in general than for ongoing operations.

Visible and specific outcomes. The outcomes or products of a project are generally more visible and specific than the outcomes of a non-project set of activities. For example, the product might be an information report, a set of policy recommendations, a program, a curriculum, curricular materials, or an activity.

Although a set of activities need not have all of these characteristics to be classed as a project, it must have most of them. The essential characteristics include clearly stated goals, time constraints, a specific and visible outcome, and a unique set of activities.

Types of Projects

Projects can be classified in several ways. Common systems include classification on the basis of methodology (e.g., survey projects, documentary studies, experimental projects), or classification according to traditional research categories (pure research, applied research, action research, development, implementation). However, we have chosen to classify projects on the basis of purpose: the major reason for conducting the set of activities. Six types of projects can be classified in this way.

1. *Information gathering.* A project is classified as "information gathering" if its major reason is to collect and present information (e.g., statistics, opinions, trends). Although the information may be analyzed and interpreted, it is not used – in the project – to evaluate programs or personnel, to develop policy alternatives, to develop programs or procedures, or to recommend courses of action.

2. *Activities.* The project mode of operation is often used to plan and conduct activities such as conferences, workshops, conventions, or short courses.

3. *Hypothesis testing.* Hypothesis testing, according to the traditional classification, is generally referred to as "pure" or "basic" research. It is used to test the relationships among variables, to confirm beliefs or the findings of other studies, and to arrive at generalizations about the relationships among variables. It can be used to generate theory or to enhance present theory. The locus of the theoretical generalizations is the researcher who arrives at, articulates, and supports the generalizations. Most hypothesis testing activities are carried out through the project mode.

4. *Policy development.* Those who govern an organization establish policies to set the direction and specify the expected outcomes of its activities. The policies do not determine the specific regulations, programs, or activities of the organization but do establish the parameters for them. In other words, policies are "guides to discretionary action." Projects are often undertaken to analyze policy and to generate alternative sets of policy directions.

5. *Product and/or program development and implementation.* Policies set the direction for the functions of an organization, but they allow for discretionary action. Therefore programs, regulations, procedures, materials, and the like must be developed or selected to implement the intent of the policy. The project mode is often used for these activities. The "D" of "R and D" represents this type of project. The implementation of a selected program, set of procedures, or materials can also be carried out through the project mode.

6. *Policy, program, and product evaluation.* The evaluation or assessment of policies, regulations, procedures, programs, and activities can also be carried out through the project mode of operation.

Projects are generally not "pure" in form; that is, they have more than one of the above six purposes. For example, while most projects include information gathering, this is not the major reason for the activity – information is gathered merely to facilitate the other purposes (for example, assessment, policy generation, or program development). Policy and program development projects generally have evaluation as a supplementary purpose, because evaluation of present policies and programs is usually necessary to test the feasibility of the alternative sets of policies or programs being generated.

The methods used to conduct the project and the sophistication of the procedures used are not governed as much by the overall purpose of the project as by the specific objectives or research questions being pursued and the conditions of the environment surrounding the project. The appropriate methods for gathering and analyzing data for a particular information gathering or implementation project may be more sophisticated than the most appropriate methods for the same functions in a particular "pure" research project. However, there are some basic differences between a hypothesis testing project and the other five discussed above.

As mentioned previously, in hypothesis testing the generation and enhancement of theory is a major purpose. The other types of projects are not intended to create or enhance theory but, rather, to use theory for the purposes of the project – assessment, policy generation, program development, and so on. In addition, in hypothesis testing the researcher is the locus of the generalizations arrived at, whereas in the other types of projects – especially evaluation, policy generation, and program development – generalization beyond the specific environment is left to the reader.

Types of Projects Usually Undertaken by School Jurisdictions

The types of projects undertaken by operational school jurisdictions usually parallel their concerns and responsibilities – policy development, program development, implementation, and evaluation. Most operating systems do not undertake hypothesis testing projects; these are left to universities and research institutes. Common types of projects include the assessment and generation of alternative policies (in a wide variety of areas such as promotions, transportation, programs, staff evaluation, or grade organization) made necessary by policy directives from a superordinate level; the development of programs to implement the intent of new policies or to take advantage of new products, information and technologies; policy, program, and personnel evaluation; and the planning and conducting of activities (e.g., conferences, conventions, workshops).

Steps Involved in Project Design and Management

Projects are usually initiated and brought to fruition through a series of steps:

1. identifying a problem or area of concern by an operating jurisdiction,
2. deciding to initiate action regarding this area of concern through the project mode,
3. deciding to carry out the project through the use of internal staff or through a contract with an external source,
4. developing specifications for the project design and operation,
5. assigning the project to internal staff or issuing a request for proposals to appropriate external sources,
6. developing a proposal by the assigned staff or interested external sources,
7. considering and accepting a proposal by the contracting agency,
8. developing the detailed management and research designs for the project by those selected or contracted to conduct it,
9. conducting the project, and
10. reporting its results.

Each of these steps is elaborated upon in the chapters which follow.

2

Project
Initiation

Projects are generally initiated because of an area of concern which some decision maker or policy maker determines should be investigated further.

Articulation of Concern

Awareness of an issue or concern needing further investigation or action may be triggered in many ways and through a wide variety of actions and circumstances. New technology or ideas presented to a conference attended by members of the school jurisdiction may create enough interest to trigger a concern about the operation of the system. Complaints from parents, teachers, students, or other stakeholders may trigger a concern about the system's programs. New policies or programs introduced by a superordinate authority (e.g., the provincial department of education) can create a need to introduce change, as can incentives such as special grants and the availability of project funding. Information gathered through a systematic monitoring and planning process can also create a need to take action to change the operation of the jurisdiction.

Before an area of concern is taken beyond the stage of awareness, two conditions must be met. First, a decision to act is made by some authority – the superintendent, the Board, a principal; second, the nature of the action is determined. The action should be articulated in general terms and should include (a) a general delineation of the area of concern (e.g., the promotion policies of the school system); (b) the background or rationale for the decision to act, (e.g., department of education statistics indicate that the system is out of step with the rest of the province and many complaints have been received from parents); (c) some general direction as to the type of investigation or further action desired (e.g., an evaluation of the present policies and practices, and the generation of alternative policies and programs); and (d) a mechanism for moving to the next stage (e.g., the superintendent is asked by the Board to develop the specifications for the project).

The type of action decided upon can take many forms: collecting information, reviewing and/or developing policies, developing a program, developing materials, creating new regulations and guidelines, evaluating a program or a policy, or providing suggestions or directives to appropriate personnel. The mode of carrying out the action may not be a project. For the purposes of this book, however, only the project mode will be considered.

The concern may be spelled out in a Board minute, a committee report, a memo from the superintendent or principal, or in many other ways depending upon the procedures used by the school jurisdiction. Regardless of the form in which the concern statement is presented, it should be prepared in such a way that positive answers are received to the following questions:

1. Is the concern statement clearly written?
2. Is the mode of action decided upon (e.g., a project) most appropriate for dealing with the area of concern?
3. If a project mode is selected, has an appropriate type of project been selected?
4. If a project mode is selected, is the necessary information included in the statement so that a request for proposal (RFP) and specification for proposal (SFP) can be prepared?

Concern Statements

The following are examples of concern statements:

Concern Statement 1. The School Board has expressed a concern regarding the issue of stress among members of the teaching profession. Recent surveys, reports, and studies have concluded that teachers experience abnormally high levels of stress, that teachers make more stress-related insurance claims than any other profession, and that a teacher's average life span is four years shorter than that of the average Canadian. The School Board has directed the Superintendent of Teacher Personnel Services to appoint a committee to conduct a thorough study of the topic. The study design would include the identification of major factors related to the levels of stress, strategies for early identification, and the provision of necessary services to counsel teachers experiencing stress nearing crises levels. The committee is responsible for preparing specifications for the study and an RFP.

Concern Statement 2. The Minister of Education indicated in a letter dated

August 28, 1985, to Board chairmen and superintendents that there is a general lack of knowledge as to how the educational system functions. He suggested that each school system set a standard of quality for a parent-student handbook. He further suggested that each school prepare a parent-student handbook to provide an accurate information base upon which parents and students can make sound educational decisions and have the foreknowledge of course expectations and student assessment procedures.

Specifications for Proposals

Before a project design and plan can be prepared, the specifications for what is wanted in any project plan must be made more elaborate than is usually the case in the concern statement. This elaboration is usually referred to as the Request for Proposal (RFP) if proposals are being requested from external persons or agencies, or as the Specification for Proposal (SFP) if the project is being conducted internally. RFP/SFPs are generally prepared by an employee or sub-group of the agency sponsoring the project – the superintendent, assistant superintendent, a principal, or a committee of teachers.

Ideally the RFP/SFP should contain statements about (1) the rationale and background for the decision to conduct the project – usually an elaboration of the concern statement; (2) the types of information wanted in the proposal – for example, title, purpose, objectives, design, time lines, management plan, budget; (3) budget constraints; (4) time constraints; (5) expected outcomes; (6) design and management constraints if any – for example, a steering committee named by the agency, hearings, no interviews; and (7) the time limit for submitting proposals. Because the RFP/SFP is the first stage in the development of a contract between the agency and those who will be conducting the project, it should spell out all of the conditions desired by the agency. This is also applicable if the project is to be conducted internally by a staff member or group of staff members. It is important that those conducting the project know as precisely as possible what is wanted by the agency. Therefore, there are very few differences between an RFP and an SFP, except for those aspects which pertain to fees and agreements between the two parties.

Those wishing to have a project conducted by an external source should be cautioned not to be too specific with respect to the design and outcomes of the project, especially if it is to be conducted by knowledgeable and experienced people. Professionals want and need considerable flexibility to develop the most appropriate design, to carry out the project in the most efficient and effective manner, and to arrive at the most defensible outcomes. If those assigned to conduct the project or to prepare proposals to conduct it are allowed considerable freedom to develop a design, the best results will be obtained. Experienced professionals will probably not bid on a project which places too many constraints on the design. An RFP/SFP is similar to a good set of policies; it is a guide to discretionary action. The agency can retain the necessary degree of control over the project through its negotiations with regard to approving the proposal and finalizing the contract, and through the monitoring and approval provisions built into the proposal. These can and should be specified in the RFP/SFP. RFP/SFPs are usually prepared by individuals or groups who have background information and a good understanding of the area of concern. Therefore, they may neglect to spell out some needed information. A good rule of thumb is for the authors of the RFP/SFP to put themselves in the position of a stranger (to both the area of concern and the agency requesting the study) who is being asked to prepare a proposal to conduct the project. By doing this, they are much more likely to spell out all the needed information and background. The following is an example of a Request for Proposal (RFP). Others may be found in Appendix A.

REQUEST FOR A PROPOSAL
EVALUATION OF THE EXTENDED CAMPUS PROGRAM

The Extended Campus Program, initiated in 1981 as a five-year pilot project funded by Advanced Education, makes it possible for students to meet their residency requirements for a Master's degree in Educational Administration in an off-campus location while holding a full-time position. The program was developed in response to a growing set of needs and demands – the inability of potential students who live some distance from the university to take advantage of the Department's Administrative Development Program, demands from school systems and educators for more feasible opportunities to pursue advanced degrees, the imbalance between the major cities and the rural areas of the province in respect to educators who hold advanced degrees, especially degrees in Educational Administration, and the willingness of several American universities to offer degree programs in sites in the northern areas of the Province.

The *purpose* of the Extended Campus Program is to provide candidates for the Master's degree in Educational Administration with an opportunity to take the residency requirements of the Program in an off-campus site, while still holding a full-time position. The program is to be equivalent to the conventional programs in respect to the ten criteria identified.

The funding contract with Advanced Education called for an external evaluation of the Project upon its termination in 1986. However, evaluative data has been collected, analyzed, and interpreted by the Project Team throughout the life of the project.

Full details of the project – its rationale, purposes, operation, and evaluation are available from the original needs assessment and proposal document, the 1984 assessment report and proposal for continuation, and from the project files which will be open to the Evaluator.

Purposes of the External Review
The purpose of the external evaluation will be to assess the project in terms of the ten criteria established, assess the accuracy and appropriateness of the internal evaluation reports, assess the desirability and feasibility of continuing the program or a similar one, and to comment on how the need which gave rise to the project might best be fulfilled.

Constraints
The following constraints will be placed on the conduct of the evaluation:

1. Participants, stakeholders, Department staff, and Project administrators must be consulted and surveyed.
2. Data must be collected from students of the ADP and conventional programs as well as from Extended Campus students.
3. The evaluator will be responsible to a Steering Committee named by the Program Coordinator.
4. The evaluation must be in terms of the ten criteria identified; however, the evaluator can include others as seem appropriate.

Expected Outcomes
The final report of the Evaluator is to include the following:

1. a statement of rationale, purposes, and study objectives;
2. methodology and design of the evaluation;
3. findings of the evaluation (analyzed data and their interpretation);
4. issues identified;
5. evaluation conclusions; and
6. recommendations for continuation and modifications.

Project Management
The conduct of the evaluation will be the responsibility of the Evaluator, under the terms contained in the evaluation agreement, which will be based on this SFP and the Proposal. The Evaluator will be responsible to the Project Coordinator through a Steering Committee named by the Coordinator. Progress reports will be made to the Steering Committee at times to be outlined in the Proposal.

Time Lines and Budget
A general plan for expenditures (which are not to exceed $15 000) is to be included in the proposal. The final report is to be presented by June 30, 1986.

The Proposal

The proposal should contain at minimum the following sections:
1. the rationale and purposes of the evaluation,
2. the objectives of the evaluation,
3. the study design (general design – details come later),
4. project management,
5. timing and phasing,
6. budget, and
7. reporting.

The evaluation proposal is to be submitted to the Project Coordinator befor September 30, 1984.

Internal or External Contracting

There are both advantages and disadvantages to having a project con ducted internally. An internal contract can be a disadvantage under two cir cumstances. (1) If the area of concern is politically sensitive, if internal peop can be accused of protecting their own interests, or if there is a chance of undue influence on internal people by superordinates or others who may hav some influence over their lives, then the project should be contracted to som external source. This is generally true with respect to policy generation pro jects, evaluation projects, and some types of program development and impl mentation projects. (2) If the area of expertise needed is not present in the ju isdiction and if the jurisdiction does not want to employ staff to institutiona ize this expertise, the same holds true. However, if these two circumstance are not a major factor, there may be financial, time, and knowledge advantag to having the project conducted internally.

There are often advantages to undertaking collaborative projects in whic the project is either conducted internally with the assistance of external con sultants and researchers, or conducted externally with the assistance of intern personnel. These arrangements are often made to optimize the advantages of both the internal and external modes of conducting projects.

If the project is to be conducted internally, the most knowledgeable an appropriate staff members should be selected or employed to conduct it. The should be given the necessary time, and they should be protected from und influence from superordinates through the same kinds of mechanisms est blished for external contracts: a contract for the project which specifies who responsible, to whom they report, and the conditions surrounding the condu

)f the project. There are no "best" methods for contracting to external sources. These lepend upon the environmental conditions surrounding the jurisdiction and he area of concern, as well as the availability of interested and knowledgeable)eople and agencies. In a particular situation it may be appropriate to ask only)ne person who is known to be an expert in the area to develop a proposal. In nother instance, it may be most appropriate to have an open competition and dvertise the RFP widely. In any case, it is very important that the time limit or submitting proposals and the address to which they are to be submitted be learly specified.

3

Proposal Preparation

Since the proposal or the overall design for a project is the foundation upon which the project must rest as well as the blueprint for conducting it, many factors must be carefully considered in developing a proposal. These are dealt with below under the headings of General Considerations, Establishing Objectives, and Overall Design. Some of the chapters which follow – The Use of Design Models, Issue Identification, Alternative Generation and Feasibility Testing, and Reporting – also contain suggestions which are useful in the proposal development stage, although they are more useful in developing the detailed project design.

General Considerations

The proposal, which contains the plan or generalized design for conducting the project, is based on the RFP/SFP but goes beyond it. Each person or agency preparing a proposal will have a particular methodological approach and an understanding of the scope and nature of the study requested; the proposal will necessarily reflect these viewpoints.

The proposal is developed by the person or group intending to conduct the project. Very seldom is this the same person or group who prepared the RFP/SFP, except in the case of a thesis proposal or a request for external research funds. In most cases the proposal is prepared in response to a written RFP/SFP obtained through the media or some other distribution system, or presented specifically to those undertaking to prepare the proposal. This latter procedure applies for most SFPs.

Stages in Designing a Project

There are usually two stages in the development of a project plan. First, the proposal forms the basis for approving the overall approach and for awarding the contract (in the case of an RFP). The second stage is the project design, which outlines the specific designs for conducting and managing the project. Although this stage is generally completed after the contract has been awarded or the general approach approved (in the case of an SFP), there are usually provisions in the proposal for having this stage approved by the contracting agency through some form of policy or steering committee. It is the proposal with which we are concerned at this time; the specific research and management designs will be discussed in other chapters.

Because the proposal is the basis for approving the overall approach and for awarding the contract, it should be completed in enough detail that the contracting agency or the employer can decide whether or not to accept it. It does not contain all specific details of research design and project management; these are usually completed after the contract is awarded.

Contents of a Proposal

A proposal generally contains the following sections, although it is the RFP/SFP which will determine the minimum contents.

Project Rationale and Purpose. The project rationale and purpose as contained in the proposal is a restatement – with appropriate elaboration and modifications – of those contained in the RFP/SFP.

Objectives. The objectives are the researcher's statements about what he or she will do, in general terms, to pursue the purposes of the project.

Project Design. The project design section of the proposal deals generally with how the objectives will be pursued.

Time Lines. The time constraints are contained in the RFP/SFP. These are restated in modified form if necessary and elaborated in the proposal.

Budget. The budget constraints are contained in the RFP/SFP. A general statement on the amount of money required for the project and how it will be expended is contained in the proposal.

Management. The person(s) or agency conducting the project, the responsible individual (director), the authority of the contractor and the contracting agency, and the specifics of reporting are contained in the management section of the proposal.

The specific nature of a proposal's contents will depend upon the type of project (information gathering, policy assessment and generation, evaluation, program development, or activity planning), the area of concern, the environmental conditions, the expertise and philosophy of the person(s) preparing the proposal, and the requirements of the RFP/SFP.

Proposal Preparation

Proposal development is generally an iterative process carried on until it is acceptable to both parties. Phone calls, visits, and possibly some preliminary investigation of the situation under study are usually necessary before a proposal is completed. The person preparing the proposal must also be able to "read" (be sensitive to) the wishes of the contracting agency. This sensitivity can be sharpened through the iterative process.

If the proposer is not known to the contracting agency or does not have a reputation in the field, it is necessary to include more details about how the project will be conducted and about the monitoring and reporting process than would be the case if the proposer were well known and had a good reputation as a researcher in the field.

Establishing Objectives

The rationale and the purposes of a project come from the contracting agency. The objectives constitute the statement of what will be done to fulfill the purposes of the project. The following four steps constitute a useful guide to developing a set of objectives for a project.

1. *Statement of Overall Purpose*

Researchers must be concerned with the rationale and purposes set out by the contracting agency, since these are the basis for the statement of objectives. The purposes stated by the contracting agency should be examined carefully and discussed with representatives of the agency to make sure that these purposes represent the real intent of the agency and that they are clear, achievable, and understood. If necessary, they should be restated to clarify and make explicit the intent of the agency. The following are appropriate types of purpose statements:

- The purpose of this study is to identify alternatives for the design, implementation, and operation of a national information management system in multicultural educational resources and materials; and to recommend the most feasible alternative.
- The purpose of the study is to examine and describe the objectives, activities, and outcomes of the Hopper Plan as these have developed and changed over time; and to consider possible alternative scheduling plans based on an examination of research and practice in scheduling, the experiences of the Hopper Plan, and the views and desires of the Board, the teaching staff, the students, and the parents.

2. *Statement of General Objectives*

After the purposes have been clarified and specified, the next major task is to spell out what the researcher plans to do to fulfill these purposes. The first step in this process is to list in general terms what must be done to fulfill the purposes of the project. No more than 10 or 12 statements should be necessary: a greater number suggests that the statements may be too specific. Statements such as the following would be appropriate:

To fulfill the purposes of this project, the following steps will be taken:

- survey other school systems about their promotions policies,
- seek the opinions of stakeholders on promotions policies,
- investigate what research has to say about promotions,
- analyze the data collected,
- interpret the data and determine the major issues,
- generate alternative promotion policies, and
- prepare a report on the project.

Note that these statements are expressed in terms of objectives – to do something. They are "what" statements, not "how" statements. For example, a statement that "opinions of stakeholders will be sought through the use of questionnaires" is not appropriate as an objective. The manner in which opinions will be sought has to do with methodology or how the objective will be pursued, not with the objective itself. Methodology comes later in the proposal. Therefore, a more appropriate objective statement would be "opinions of stakeholders will be sought."

3. *Statement of Specific Objectives*

There should be objectives concerning each major phase of the project. For example, in a policy or program development project there should be objectives for each of the following phases: designing the project, gathering data, analyzing data, interpreting the data, preparing the case or story (the findings), identifying issues, developing policies (and/or programs, etc.), making recommendations, and reporting.

In some studies it may be appropriate to have more than one objective for each phase, and in some cases one objective may be used to cover more than one phase. However, it is important that all phases be accounted for in the objective statements. The following example illustrates the difference between a statement of *overall purpose* and statements of *specific objectives:*

Overall Purpose

The purpose of the Plan Development Project is to give overall direction and a structure to the future development of the Valley Institute of Technology, through the development of alternative general plans in the areas of (1) program, (2) program delivery, (3) governance and management structures and styles affecting program development and delivery, and (4) program financing.

Specific Objectives

1. Designing the project: "to develop a detailed design for the conduct of the study,"
2. Gathering data: "to identify the research findings and practices in other jurisdictions which pertain to the mission established for the Institute,"
3. Analyzing data: "to analyze, collate, and synthesize the data gathered,"
4. Interpreting the data: "to interpret the data analyzed,"
5. Preparing the case or story: "to prepare the findings of the study,"
6. Identifying issues: "to identify the issues which must be resolved or be taken into account by the Institute as it moves toward its program, delivery, governance, and financing goals,"
7. Developing policies, programs, etc: "to generate and test for feasibility a set of alternative programs, program delivery systems, systems for program coordination, and governance and financing structures,"
8. Making recommendations: "to develop a set of recommendations in respect to the most appropriate policy plan,"
9. Reporting: "to prepare and present a report to the Board of the Institute in respect to the purposes and objectives of this study."

A preliminary investigation of the literature and the selection or development of a conceptual framework to guide the design and conduct of your study will also help determine the specific objectives. These are dealt with in the next chapter.

4. *Validation of Objectives*

The objectives should be validated by asking two questions. If I do everything I have said I will do, will I have fulfilled the purposes of the project? If I do everything I have said I will do, will there be anything left to do to finish the project? If the answer to the first question is "yes" and the answer to the second question is "no," the set of objectives is probably valid.

The objectives constitute the foundation and the keystone for the entire project: everything else is built upon them or held up by them. If something is missing in the objectives, it will be missing from the project.

Overall Design

The design is the researcher's plan for doing the things specified in the objectives statements. The design will vary from project to project depending upon (a) the type of project being planned (policy analysis, program development, evaluation, information gathering, or activities planning); (b) the environment surrounding the area of concern (type of data needed, sources of data, nature of the context, political sensitivity, etc.); (c) the conceptual framework(s) selected; and (d) the philosophy and modes of operation of the researcher.

Basic Design Components

Although the design may vary from project to project and from situation to situation, there are some basic components which must be in any design: (a) overall phasing and timing of the project; (b) selection of a conceptual framework(s) and specification of sub-objectives or research questions; (c) data collection; (d) data analysis; (e) interpretation and presentation of findings; (f) issue identification, if it is appropriate for the type of project; (g) alternative development, if it is appropriate for the type of project; (h) recommendation formulation, if it is appropriate for the type of project; (i) project management; and (j) reporting.

Specificity of Design

The specificity of the design in the proposal document depends upon several factors: (a) the specifications in the RFP/SFP (some RFP/SFPs demand greater specification of design than do others); (b) the nature of the project (in some types of projects the appropriate methodology is known, as are the instruments to be used; in such cases the design can be very specific); and (c) the credibility of the researcher (if the researcher is not known to the contracting agency or does not have a reputation as a researcher in the substantive or methodological field of the project, the design must be more specific than it might otherwise have to be). However, in most cases the design can and should be fairly general and flexible. This allows for modifications which seem necessary and desirable in the light of new data and circumstances which arise during the life of a project.

The first phase of any project after mobilization should be project design. This phase should start early and continue until near the end of the project. This allows for the flexibility required in most projects to modify procedures in light of new information and circumstances. On the other hand, the general design contained in the proposal should be specific enough that the contracting agency can decide whether or not the researcher understands the concern and the situation, understands appropriate design systems and methodologies, and is competent in the area. Therefore, at minimum, each aspect of the design should contain (a) the alternative approaches being considered; (b) the most probable approaches in light of the present knowledge and circumstances; and (c) the procedures which will be used to finalize the design and seek the approval of or at least feedback from the contracting agency.

The proposals in Appendix B illustrate appropriate design statements for the types of project proposals described in this book.

4
The Use
of Design Models

Conceptual and analytical models drawn from the literature or developed specifically for the purposes of a project can be very useful in project design and management. The word "model" refers to a simplified representation of reality or a portion of reality. (A model is often called a "framework" if it is used as a major guide in conducting the study or a significant part of it.) A model can be used to determine the approach to the project, to describe the overall design and the procedures for collecting and analyzing data, to identify issues, to generate and test alternatives, and to develop recommendations.

Models are used in two ways in the design and conduct of projects: first, to assist in describing and understanding the phenomenon being studied and, second, to predict behavior if possible. The "Social Systems Model" represents one perception of how organizations are structured and how they function; the "Force Field Model" suggests how change occurs in organizations; and the "Situational Leadership Model" is a conceptualization of effective leadership in organizations. Since these types of models are most often derived from the literature (theory and research in the field), they are referred to as "theoretical" or "conceptual" models. Model building and testing is, in fact, theory building. Theoretical models consist of parts (concepts) and the relationships among these parts (structure). Therefore, they can and often are used for predictive purposes. For example, if we know how an organization is made up, what the interrelationships of its parts are, and how it relates to its environment, then we can predict that if "A" occurs (e.g., oxygen is taken away from a flame), "B" will follow (e.g., the flame will go out).

In building a conceptual model, one sets up an analogy between a relatively well-known and well-understood set of parts and relationships – say, a biological organism – and a relatively unknown and little understood set of parts and relationships – say, a social organization. The social organization can then be described and explained in terms of the biological organism. Poets and philosophers have been doing this for centuries: in *Coriolanus,* Shakespeare compares the political state to the human body; in *The Republic,* Plato compares our concept of the ideal world to shadows on the wall of a cave. Creating a model helps in suggesting and testing interrelationships. However, it can also act as a deterrent to finding a better fit between "our understanding" and "reality," because analogies are never exact correlations, and because once a model is selected, the researcher may use it as a blinder and therefore may not be open to other ways of viewing the phenomenon under study.

The word "model" can also be defined as a map or a pattern to follow in planning or conducting a project or parts of the project; such maps are called process models. Used in this way, as is also the case with conceptual models, the model does not attempt to depict everything in the environment, but only those aspects of concern to the researcher for the purposes of his or her project. For example, a road map is not a realistic representation of everything the traveler will see and experience while moving through the country. It includes only those features of most value to the traveler for the purposes he or she has in mind. Therefore, different models are necessary to represent different aspects of the environment (reality), depending upon the needs of the user.

As suggested in Chapter 1, projects of the type dealt with in this book (policy and program analysis, evaluation, and development) are theory based. That is, they use theory to assist in describing, analyzing, assessing, and solving the problems being investigated. Therefore, the use of theoretical or conceptual models is very appropriate for designing and conducting projects. They can provide clues and guidelines for developing objectives and sub-objectives (research questions), for the overall approach to designing the study, for identifying sources and means of collecting and analyzing data, for interpreting data and presenting findings, for identifying issues, for generating and testing alternatives, and for developing conclusions and/or recommendations. Process models are also very useful as frameworks for organizing, planning, and managing the project, for collecting and analyzing data, and for reporting findings.

The sections which follow deal with the use of general design models, process models, special purpose models, and data-gathering frameworks.

General Design Models

A "general design model" provides an overall set of concepts for the study. It suggests the theoretical basis for approaching the problem being investigated and also provides a framework for developing research questions, data gathering procedures, data analysis, issue generation, and alternative development. General design models can be very broad in scope – the "Social Systems Model" – or they can be selected for a narrow purpose – the "Stake Model" for program evaluation. Appropriate models from the literature can be used for general design purposes (for example, the Social Systems Model and the Stake Model), or models can be constructed, using appropriate concepts from the literature, for the special purposes of the study.

Use of the Social Systems Model: An Illustration

Social systems theory, which is based on a biological systems model, suggests that all organizations have a purpose or reason for being, that they are made up of parts, that these parts are more closely related to one another with respect to the purposes of the organization than they are to elements in the environment, that the behavior of one part of the organization affects the other parts and the organization as a whole, and that the organization takes in resources (inputs) from its environment which it processes and then returns to the environment in a modified form (outputs). There also exists a feedback mechanism, from the environment to the organization and from each part of the organization to the other parts, which acts to monitor and control the operations of the organization. The theory also contains many predictive concepts respecting the relationships of the organization to its environment, the relationships among parts of the organization, and the overall behavior of the organization. Figure 1 illustrates the basic components and relationships in a social system. A complete discussion of social systems theory can be found in Beishon and Peters (1976), von Bertalanffy (1968), and van Gigch (1978).

Figure 2 illustrates how Miklos, Ingram, and McIntosh (1971) applied the Social Systems Model in designing their study of the Yellowhead School Division. This model was used to identify the components and relationships in the Division which should be examined. It was also used as a guide to suggest possible relationships within the school system and between the system and its environment.

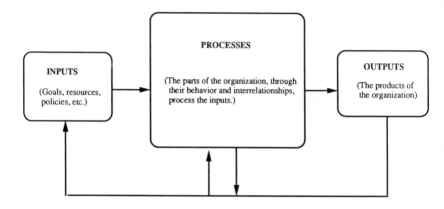

Figure 1

Social Systems Model

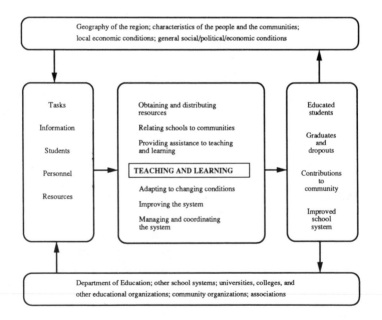

Figure 2

**System View of the Operation
of a School District**

Use of the Stake Model: An Illustration

Robert Stake (1967) developed a conceptual model designed to guide the evaluation of new programs and procedures to be introduced into an organization. His model is based on the assumption that the evaluation process is determined and put into place before a program is introduced, although the model can be used to guide the evaluation design for other types of programs as well. Therefore, for projects of this nature the Stake Model may be an appropriate one to use – provided the researcher and the client system agree with its underlying values and assumptions.

Figure 3 depicts the type of data to be collected and the planning to be done in order to conduct the type of evaluation conceptualized in the Stake Model.

The "Descriptive Matrix" in the Stake Model is made up of six cells. The three cells in the left-hand column represent observations or the collection of information about the "intents" or plans for the new program before it is implemented. The three cells in the right-hand column represent observations of what has actually been introduced or what takes place after the program has been implemented. Observations can be made at different time intervals. The top row of cells in the Descriptive Matrix represents what was intended and observed to be in place before the program was introduced. For example, in a teacher aide program it might have been intended to have in place three aides, all with formal preparation; a program and a guidebook for teachers on the use of aides; a job description for the aides; and a teaching staff which supported the introduction of the program. However, it might be observed three months after the program is introduced that only two aides – only one with formal preparation – have been employed, that the staff have not been prepared and are only partially supportive of the program, and that no job descriptions have been prepared. The center row represents the transactions (activities, relationships, behaviors, etc.) which make up the program, and the bottom row represents the intended and observed outcomes of the program.

The "Judgment Matrix" is also made up of six cells. The three cells in the left-hand column represent the standards established for acceptable antecedents, transactions, and outcomes. The three cells in the right-hand column represent the procedures for making judgments respecting the evaluation of the program – antecedents, transactions, and outcomes.

The twelve cells in Figure 3 plus the "Rationale" box can be used as a guide in developing research questions, in determining an overall approach to the project, and in designing the data gathering system.

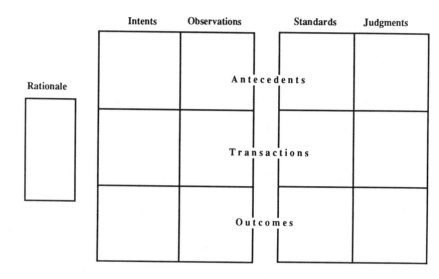

Figure 3

**A Layout of Statements and Data to be Collected
by an Evaluator of an Educational Program
(Stake Model)**

Figure 4 depicts the concepts included in the model regarding the analysis of the data collected. Three types of analysis are included. The first is an examination of the logical contingency between the intended antecedents and the intended transactions, and between the intended transactions and the intended outcomes. In other words, is it logical to expect the intended transactions to take place from the intended antecedents, and is it logical to expect the intended outcomes from the intended transactions? It would not be logical to expect aides to help the students with problems in algebra – an intended transaction – if an intended antecedent was to employ aides who did not require knowledge of or formal preparation in the areas covered by their job descriptions.

The second type of analysis is to examine empirically the relationships between the observed antecedents and the observed transactions, and between the observed transactions and the observed outcomes. The third type of analysis is to examine the congruence between the intents and the observations – antecedents, transactions, and outcomes.

Descriptive Data

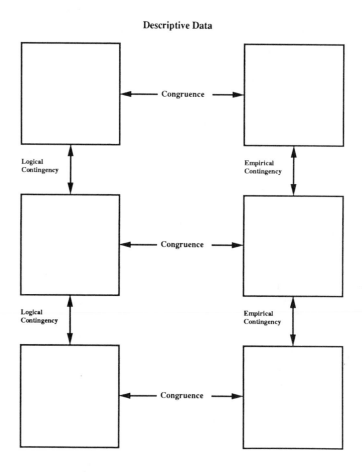

Figure 4

**A Representation of the Processing
of Descriptive Data
(Stake Model)**

Figure 5 illustrates one method for making judgments about the program being evaluated: the descriptive data from the program being evaluated are compared with the descriptive data from a "comparison program" and with the acceptable standards selected. Other procedures for making judgments may also be appropriate. Who makes the judgments, and what criteria are used for making them, also have to be decided by the evaluator.

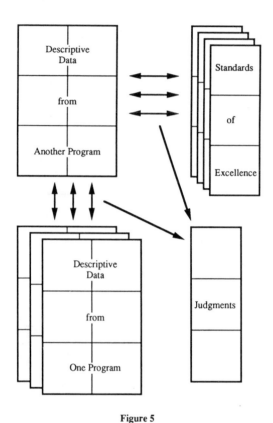

Figure 5

**A Representation of the Process of Judging
the Results of an Educational Program
(Stake Model)**

Several other models for guiding evaluation projects exist, as do models for guiding other types of projects; the Stake Model was described for illustrative purposes only. The models selected must be appropriate for the purposes of the study and must be acceptable to the researcher and to the client. It is also appropriate to use one model for some purposes but not for others. For example, the Stake Model might be used to guide the data gathering process, but not the analysis; other models might be selected or developed for this purpose. If two or more models are used to guide different aspects of the project, it is important that they be compatible in respect to the basic concepts included.

Researcher Developed Models: Two Illustrations

Appropriate models may not exist in the literature. In such cases the researcher is obliged to develop his or her own model(s) for guiding the study. The concepts selected for inclusion in these models must be compatible (based upon acceptable knowledge) and appropriate for the purposes for which they are being used.

The model depicted in Figure 6 was developed to guide data collection for a superintendency study (Downey, 1973). The selection of the components of the "Positional Variables" matrix was based on the literature. The components of the "Situational Variables" matrix were selected partially on the basis of the literature and partially because of the requirements of the RFP. The components of the "Time Period" matrix were requested in the RFP. A data-gathering system was developed to collect the appropriate data for each of the 60 cells in the model.

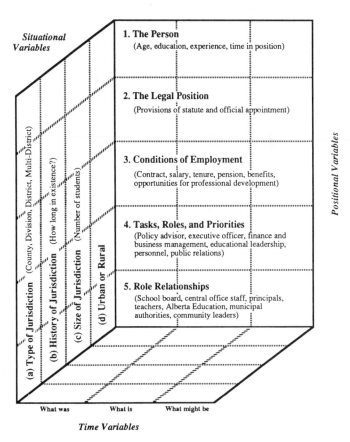

Figure 6

The Superintendency: A Conceptual Framework

The Layered Component Model depicted in Figure 7 was developed by the author for a project which had as its purpose the development of a system evaluation design for the County of Strathcona Board of Education (Ingram, 1984). It provides a conceptual framework which could be used to determine the overall approach to system evaluation, program evaluation, and school evaluation for any school jurisdiction. It also provides a framework for determining the components to be reviewed, the depth of the review of

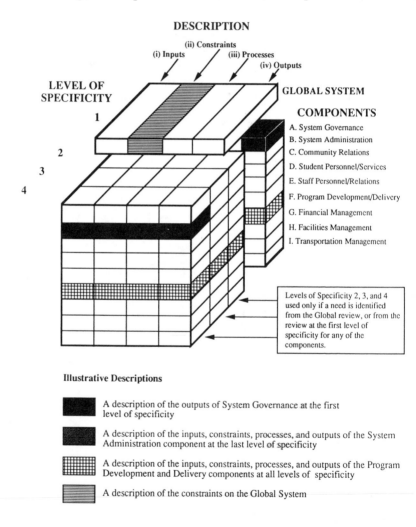

DESCRIPTION

(ii) Constraints
(i) Inputs   (iii) Processes
(iv) Outputs

LEVEL OF
SPECIFICITY

GLOBAL SYSTEM

COMPONENTS

A. System Governance
B. System Administration
C. Community Relations
D. Student Personnel/Services
E. Staff Personnel/Relations
F. Program Development/Delivery
G. Financial Management
H. Facilities Management
I. Transportation Management

Levels of Specificity 2, 3, and 4 used only if a need is identified from the Global review, or from the review at the first level of specificity for any of the components.

Illustrative Descriptions

A description of the outputs of System Governance at the first level of specificity

A description of the inputs, constraints, processes, and outputs of the System Administration component at the last level of specificity

A description of the inputs, constraints, processes, and outputs of the Program Development and Delivery components at all levels of specificity

A description of the constraints on the Global System

Figure 7
Layered Component Model for System
Evaluation: Strathcona Application

any of the components, and a structure for describing the components selected for review. The model is based partially on the modeling approach to program evaluation developed by Borich and Jemelka (1982). Specific guidelines are not provided beyond the description of the components or transactions selected for review. Other models need to be selected or developed to guide the delimitation of indicators and standards, the collection and analysis of data, the interpretation of data, the judgment of merit, and the presentation of findings.

The Description Dimension. The horizontal or description dimension of the Layered Component Model suggests that the description of the school system and its components (e.g., Governance, Administration, Program, Student Services, etc.) be in terms of the inputs, transactions, outputs, and constraints as conceptualized in systems theory, and especially as elaborated by Borich and Jemelka. The specific types of data to be collected will vary depending upon the component being reviewed. For example, the types of data to be collected to describe the Governance component of the school system will be much different from those gathered to describe the Student Services component. What the Layered Component Model suggests is that a complete evaluation will require information on the inputs, constraints, processes, and outputs of the component under review.

The Component Dimension. The vertical or component dimension of the Layered Component Model suggests that an evaluation can be made of (1) the Global System, illustrated by the top-separated slice; (2) any of the components or parts of the system, illustrated by the lower nine connected slices; or (3) any combination of these components.

The Layered Component Model is flexible in terms of the categorization of system components and sub-components. A categorization system which best fits the structure of the particular school system would be most appropriate. For example, the Operational Handbook for the Strathcona School System categorizes the policies according to the following system:

A. Foundations and Basic Commitments

B. Board Governance and Operations

C. General School Administration

D. Business Administration

E. Support Services

F. Facilities Development

G. Personnel

H. Curriculum and Instruction

I. Students

J. School/Community Relations

Other models might also be appropriate as a guide: Miklos (1975) and Miklos, Ingram and McIntosh (1971). Other categorization systems might also be developed. This decision rests with the Evaluator and/or the Policy Committee of the school system for which it is being designed. However, the categorization system used should cover all possible activities and components contained in the school system under review.

The Levels of Specificity Dimension. The depth or levels of specificity dimension of the Layered Component Model provides for the layered approach from which the model gets its name. It allows for the systematic breakdown of system components into sub-components or layers. The depth of investigation of any one component is to be decided by the Evaluator and/or the Policy Committee responsible for the review. The depth of the initial investigation can be decided at the beginning of the evaluation project, or it can be delayed until evaluative data on the first layer of specificity are analyzed.

The Curriculum and Instruction classifications in the County of Strathcona Operational Handbook will serve as an illustration of the layered process:

Level 1: Curriculum and Instruction

- School Year
- School Day
- Curriculum Development
- Curriculum Design
- Instructional Arrangements
- Instructional Resources
- Guidance and Counselling Programs
- Testing Programs
- Evaluation of Instruction

Level 2: Instructional Resources

- Instructional Materials
- Instructional Services

Level 3: Instructional Services

- In-School Classified Staff
- Learning Resource Services
- Teacher Center

– Field Trips
– Volunteer Help in Schools

Level 4:

(Further breakdowns as necessary)

During any particular review the Evaluator and/or the System Steering Committee may decide to stop at Level 1 for one component and go to Level 4 for another.

Process Models

The term "process model" as used in this book refers to a guide or framework for developing the structure of the project and for determining the processes of planning and conducting the study. It includes the major aspects of the study and the relationships among these aspects. The concepts and structures basic to the process models illustrated in Figures 8, 9, and 10 were developed by the author in the order presented over a period of several years. They are based partially on the literature in the fields of policy analysis, planning, and change, and partially on the experiences of the author and his colleagues in designing and conducting projects.

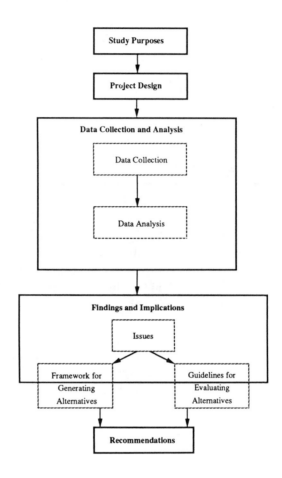

Figure 8

Project Design Model (1)

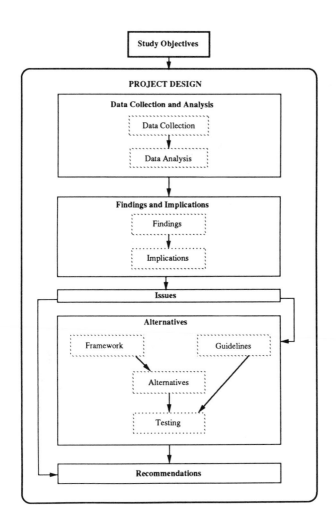

Figure 9

Project Design Model (2)

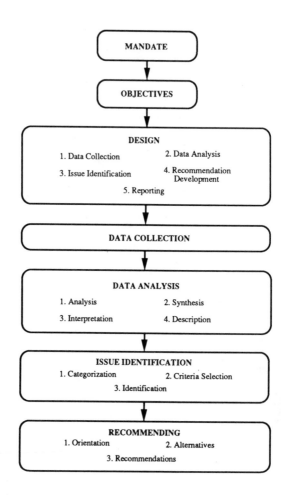

Figure 10

Project Design Model (3)

Several concepts are embedded in these models. First, there are six major phases to any evaluation, policy analysis, or program development project: (1) design of all phases of the project; (2) data collection and analysis; (3) development of the findings and their implications; (4) issue identification; (5) generation of conclusions, alternative solutions, and recommendations; and (6) reporting. Second, the identification of the issues surrounding any problem is necessary in order to generate appropriate and feasible conclusions. Third, it is important to generate and test for feasibility (theoretical at least) more than one possible alternative solution (policy, program, conclusion, recommendation) in order to increase the confidence in the stated recommendations and to give the client a greater range of choices. Fourth, each phase of the project is based upon the findings and experiences of the previous phases. Last, the key phases of any project are the design, the development of implications, the identification of issues, and the generation of conclusions.

Although the type of process model illustrated in Figures 8, 9, and 10 has proven effective, other models could be developed which could be just as effective.

Special Purpose Models

In addition to the process model used to guide the structure of the project, and the general design model(s) used to determine the substantive approach and research design, other models can be selected for special purposes – for example, data analysis and alternative generation.

An Illustrative Example

The Stress Model depicted in graphic form in Figure 11 was applied by the author and his colleagues in conducting an evaluation of an instructional model introduced into a new community college. A preliminary analysis of the data collected, using the Stake Model as a guide, revealed the existence of a great deal of stress in the college. Therefore, it was deemed appropriate to use a stress model to analyze and interpret the data further, to guide the identification of issues, and to give clues as to alternative solutions to the problems identified. The model selected was one developed by Selye (1974) to describe, explain, and predict stress in human beings. However, because of the precedence of systems theory and other theoretical constructs concerning organizational behavior, it was considered appropriate to extend the model to examine stress in organizations.

Data Collection Models

Another type of model, similar in many respects to a process model but designed for only one aspect of the design and conduct of a project, is a data collection model or, more appropriately, a data collection framework. The type of data collection framework illustrated in Tables 1 and 2 in Appendix C was developed by the author over a period of years. The basis of the framework is the set of project objectives. For each objective, the framework provides the researcher with a means of identifying the data needed and their sources or location. It also requires the researcher to decide on the means of collecting each type of data and on the specific administration procedures. The researcher who completes all sections of the framework has completely designed the means and procedures for collecting all the data necessary for each project objective. The frameworks in Tables 1 and 2 in Appendix C illustrate how each was used in specific projects.

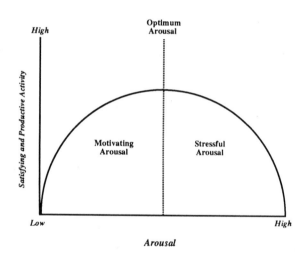

Figure 11

Organizational Stress:
A Conceptual Framework

(Based on Selye, 1974)

A Guide to the Use of Models

Although models and frameworks are necessary and can be very helpful in the design and conduct of projects, they can also be frustrating to apply or unproductive; they may even lead to false conclusions if inappropriately selected and applied. Therefore, a great deal of care must be taken in selecting, developing, and applying models and frameworks.

The following questions might well be asked before a decision is made to apply a particular model selected from the literature or developed specifically for the purposes of the project.

- Will the model be useful for the purpose for which it was selected?
- Is the model comprehensible?
- Can the model be supported theoretically and/or empirically?
- Is the model appropriate – that is, does it fit the uses to which it will be put?
- If more than one model is used, are they compatible?

5

Detailed Design:
Data Collection,
Analysis, and Findings

The first set of tasks following approval of the project proposal and (if appropriate) finalization of the contract is developing a detailed design for the study. As suggested earlier, this design phase will probably be spread throughout the project.

Data Collection

The first step in developing a detailed design for the project is to design the data collection system. The two data collection models discussed in Chapter 4 are used as a framework for a discussion of this process. These models suggest four stages to designing a data collection system: (1) determining data needs; (2) identifying the sources of data; (3) deciding on the means of collecting data; and (4) administering the collection of data.

Data Needs

The data needs for any project originate from the purposes and objectives of the project, the conceptual model(s) selected to guide the research process, and a preliminary review of the literature. Therefore, the first step following the determination of objectives is to conduct a preliminary review of the literature and practice in the area of study. The selection or development of the conceptual framework for the study, if not already determined, may well grow out of this review. The project objectives and the information obtained from the preliminary review of the literature can then be used as the basis for developing a list of sub-objectives or research questions. The following excerpts (from a proposal to conduct a study of multicultural information systems) illustrate the nature of

43

research questions.

DESIGN OF THE STUDY

During this phase of the study, research questions and possible sources of data will be identified. A preliminary investigation has identified a number of research questions for each of the objectives.

1. *To determine the extent of resources and materials in Canada in multicultural education.*

   a. What types of materials exist?
   b. What other resources exist (people, organizations)?
   c. Who holds and/or collects such materials or compiles information on such resources and materials?
   d. What mechanisms exist or are being planned for collecting, describing, and sharing such information?
   e. What significant material from other countries is collected, by whom is it collected, and what are the procedures for sharing such materials?

2. *To identify and describe appropriate existing information management systems capable of supporting a database of resources and materials, resource and information centres and agencies, or resource persons.*

   a. What systems exist?
   b. What type of information does each include?
   c. How is the information and/or material collected for each system?
   d. How is the information classified within each system?
   e. How is information added, modified, searched, and reported for each system?
   f. What are the implementation and operational costs for each system?
   g. How is each system funded?

3. *To develop a set of requirements for a national information management system in multicultural educational resources and materials.*

   Collector requirements:

   a. Who is to collect and/or hold the material?
   b. What materials and resources are to be collected?
   c. How are material and resources to be identified and gathered (solicitation, purchase, etc.)?
   d. Is collecting a voluntary effort or financially supported and by whom is it to be supported?
   e. Who is responsible for loaning or sharing of material collected?

   Indexer requirements:

   a. Who will be responsible for indexing (e.g., same body as collector)?
   b. What bibliographic standard should be used?
   c. What will be the method of indexing: fixed or free vocabulary, PRECIS, classification system, etc.?

d. Will abstracts be included, and who will be responsible for writing them if included?
e. What is the financial support for indexing activities?

Data entry requirements:

a. Who is responsible for data entry?
b. In what format is information received from indexer?
c. What is the standard of accuracy?
d. What are the data entry procedures and practices?
e. What is the financial support for data entry activity, including system costs?

Editor requirements:

a. Who should be responsible for overall editing, maintenance, production and coordination of the database?
b. What are those responsibilities?
c. What is the method of and standard for indexing and data entry?
d. What are the formats of output?
e. What is the production policy?
f. What is the financial support for editorial functions?

Consumer requirements:

a. Who will be the consumers of these data?
b. Where are these consumers located?
c. What is the current knowledge/usage level of computer systems by the consumers?
d. What access do the consumers have to computer systems?
e. What access to, and familiarity with, existing information management systems do these consumers have?
f. What kinds of resources and materials would the consumers require in an information management system?
g. How would the consumers like information to be indexed?
h. How would the consumers prefer to search for information?
i. In what language(s) would the consumers like information to be stored?
j. In what language(s) would the consumers like information to be searched?

4. *To identify possible sources and amounts of funding for the development, implementation and operation of a national information management system in multicultural educational resources and materials.*

a. What funding might be available, and from what sources, to develop and implement the system?
b. What funding might be available, and from what sources, to operate the system?
c. Should a "charge for service" policy be implemented?

. To develop a prototype management information system(s) which includes features of the alternative(s).

    a. What features can/should be included?

    b. What are the associated costs?

6. *To assess the feasibility of each of the possible systems in relation to user requirements and financial resources.*

    a. What are the costs of alternative systems?

    b. How well do alternative systems meet the user needs?

    c. How easy to use are the alternatives?

    d. How workable are the alternatives?

7. *To recommend an appropriate information management system which best suits the needs of the user group.*

    a. Which of the alternatives is the most feasible?

8. *To recommend mechanisms and procedures for the design, implementation, and operation of the recommended system.*

    a. How might the system be implemented?

    b. How might the system be operated?

The only difference between a research question and a sub-objective is in wording. For example, the research question "What types of materials exist?" could be stated in the form of a sub-objective, "to determine the types of materials which exist."

The data needs for any project constitute the information needed to satisfactorily answer the research questions or to reach the sub-objectives. For example, in Table 2, Appendix C, the data needed to "monitor the operations of Education North in respect to its structures, functions, activities and relationships" included documents, minutes, letters, etc. related to the operation of Education North; the recollections and views of involved individuals; and reports on the activities of the project.

In determining data needs, there must be some likelihood that the information included in the "needs" list exists, that it can be obtained, and that it would contribute to answering the research question. Care must also be taken to ensure that all information necessary to answer the research question has been considered.

Sources of Data

There are only four basic sources of information: (1) information storage systems such as libraries and data banks, (2) the files and records of organizations and individuals, (3) the minds of people, and (4) the activities and behavior of people and organizations.

In identifying the specific data sources in information storage systems and in sets of files and documents from organizations and individuals, the researcher must ensure that the full range of appropriate data is searched, that the information is accessible, and that the reliability and validity of the data and the sources are investigated.

In planning the collection of information from the minds of people, the researcher must take care to include the appropriate groups of people in the population to be surveyed, use appropriate sampling techniques, and check the accessibility of the information.

Means of Collecting Data

There are also only four basic means of collecting data: (1) library and document searches, (2) questionnaires and opinionnaires, (3) interviews, and (4) observations. However, there is a wide range of techniques and processes for collecting data by each of these means. Usually, data which exist in information storage systems are best obtained through library and document searches; data which exist in the minds of people are best obtained through questionnaires, opinionnaires and interviews; and data which exist in the behaviors and interrelationships of people are best obtained through observations and interviews.

Whichever means and techniques are used to collect data, these techniques should be tested for appropriateness (will they produce the information needed?), validity (will they collect accurate information?), and reliability (will they produce the same results on repeated administrations?). If the use of questionnaires, opinionnaires, or interviews is selected, the existence of suitable instruments which have already been tested for validity and reliability should be investigated before new instruments are constructed.

The collection of appropriate, reliable, and accurate data requires a wide range of knowledge and a complex set of skills on the part of the responsible researchers. Therefore, this area of research methodology should be thoroughly investigated before a decision is made as to data collection procedures. Several good references are available: Bogdan and Biklen (1982); Borg and Gall (1983); Bradburn, Sudman, and Associates (1979); Federal Statistical Activities Secretariat (1979); Kerlinger (1979); Orlich (1978); Simon and Boyer (1970); and Sudman and Bradburn (1983).

Administration of Data Collection

Data are collected from individuals and organizations. Therefore, in order to increase the likelihood of obtaining accurate and reliable data, the researcher must, first, take care to gain access to these sources at times which are convenient to the data source and in such a way that mutual trust and cooperation are obtained and maintained; second, select the time and procedures for collecting data so as to maximize the likelihood of obtaining the best and most accurate data; and, third, inform all involved parties about the proposed procedures.

As previously mentioned, it is also important when using question-naires, opinionnaires, and interviews to select the appropriate size of sample using acceptable sampling techniques. Several good references on sampling are available, including Erickson and Nosanchuk (1977) and Ferguson (1976).

Data Analysis

Data analysis involves treating or processing the data in such a way that they become meaningful or can be used to answer the research questions. Therefore, the system(s) for data analysis and for data collection should be determined at the same time.

Several factors should be kept in mind in designing the data analysis system(s). First, the analysis should be based on the purposes of the study, the objectives, and the research questions. In other words, the information obtained should assist the researcher in solving the problems being investi-gated. Second, the analysis does not constitute the findings of the study. It merely treats the data in such a way that they are more meaningful in terms of the purposes of the study. The analyzed data are used in arriving at the study findings. Finally, there are many methods of and devices for data analysis. Make sure that the methods and models selected are appropriate for the study and for the data being analyzed.

As was the case with respect to data collection methods, the appropriate and accurate analysis of data requires a wide range of knowledge and a complex set of skills on the part of responsible researchers. Therefore, this area of research methodology should be thoroughly investigated before a decision is made as to data analysis procedures. Several good references are available: Bogdan and Biklen (1982); Borg and Gall (1983); Kerlinger (1979); and Kidder (1981).

Study Findings

The study findings consist of (1) a description of the situation, problem or issue under investigation; (2) a presentation of the analyzed data in terms of the purposes and objectives of the study and the research questions or sub-objectives used to guide the collection and analysis of data (including the literature review and any document analysis); (3) a synthesis of all sets of data collected and analyzed; and (4) an interpretation of the data in terms of the purposes and objectives of the study.

An Approach to Developing the Findings

Researchers should adopt the perspective of an impartial observer when preparing to produce and present findings. This is a very difficult perspective to adopt, especially if the researchers are involved in the situation under study or have firm opinions about the subject or the situation – as is likely the case for the types of projects discussed in this book. Therefore, from the point of view of both credibility and the validity of the findings, it is important for researchers to bring their biases into the open and deal with them. Researchers can do this by thinking through and listing their biases and then participating in a seminar where the possible biases are discussed, along with possible means of dealing with them in the interpretation of the data. The use of other people in data analysis and interpretation, preferably ones who have different perspectives from those of the researchers, is one means of dealing with researcher bias; the "bouncing off" process is particularly effective in this situation. In addition to these procedures, both the findings and the interpretations should be properly critiqued by knowledgeable individuals at "arm's length" from the research team.

Presentation of Findings

Three types of statements can be found in the presentation of findings: facts, dynamics, and interpretations.

Facts. A fact is usually something that is directly observable and accepted by most people if appropriate evidence is presented. For example, the statements "The system is composed of 12 schools and 200 teachers" and "Eighty-four per cent of the teachers claimed to be satisfied with the evaluation system" are considered statements of fact if there is supporting evidence.

Dynamics. "Dynamics" statements suggest relationships and/or movements which are not directly observable: they are implied from the facts. For example, the statements "the principals are satisfied with the reporting system used" and "the orientation of the people in the district is becoming more urban" are considered "dynamics." Most stakeholders are willing to accept dynamics statements if they are closely related to the facts as presented. However, because they are not directly observable, there may be more doubt in the minds of the originating committee.

Interpretations. Interpretations of facts and dynamics must be made in terms of the purposes, objectives, and research questions. They are one step further removed from observability than are the dynamics. For example, the statements "the instructional system of the Division has improved over the last five years" and "the attendance area policy of the Division is creating concern and conflict in the area" are considered interpretations. Because they are further removed from observability, they are generally relationship or cause-and-effect oriented, and they must be tied directly to the purposes of the study. They are more open to doubt, disagreement, and debate than are statements of fact or dynamics.

In presenting the findings, the researcher should make it clear that a statement is a fact, a dynamic, or an interpretation. Interpretations and dynamics should not be presented as facts. It is also important that the dynamics and the interpretations flow from the facts, and that they be supported by evidence presented in the report.

6

Issue
Identification

Chapter 5 stressed that the findings and interpretations of them constitute the major set of data to be used by the researcher in moving toward the final stage of the study – conclusions as to the assessment of a program, a set of policy recommendations, or a new program. However, the issues present in the situation must be identified before one can proceed to the final stage in most policy, development, and evaluation studies.

Definition

Webster's Collegiate Dictionary (Seventh Edition) defines the word "issue" as "a matter that is in dispute between two or more parties. . . . a point of debate or controversy. . . . [a matter] under discussion or debate. . . . a matter] in a state of controversy. . . . a point at which an unsettled matter is ready for decision."

Issues can be defined only in terms of what they relate to. For example, in a study of an educational organization, issues are defined in terms of one or more components of the organization – its mandate, mission, purposes, programs, organization, adaptive and coordinating mechanisms, internal relationships, external relationships, services, products, organizational health, or the relationships among these components. Therefore, an issue exists when the purposes or operations of the organization (or one or more of its components) are unsettled or in dispute, or even in a state of turbulence; or when various environmental factors are seen to constrain desired modifications in the operations of the organization.

Varying combinations of factors may contribute to the creation of any issue: opposing positions taken by members of the organization and/or its stakeholders; changing needs and demands; technological changes; changes

51

in the knowledge base; shifts in the philosophical or political climate; tradition; inertia; and/or changes in human and economic support.

The following excerpt from a study of a faculty of education illustrates what is meant by the term "issue."

> One issue confronting the Faculty, which is directly related to mandate and organization and indirectly related to many other components of the Faculty, is the overall conceptual model which drives the Faculty, its departments, and its members. That is, to what extent should the Faculty be driven by a "professional" model as opposed to a "liberal studies," "academic," or "discipline" model? For the purposes of this illustration, the "professional" model might be described as one which places major emphasis on the preparation and updating of members of a profession and on collaboration with the profession in solving problems related to the practice of the profession – medicine, law, nursing, agriculture, engineering, education – and which therefore organizes itself and its rewards system with these major purposes in mind. The "discipline" mode, on the other hand, places major emphasis on developing and passing on knowledge about the discipline – mathematics, chemistry, history – and therefore organizes itself and its rewards system with this purpose in mind. The traditional "liberal studies" model applied by the arts and science faculties in most universities is typical of a "discipline" model.
>
> Although the "professional" model governs some aspects of the operation of the Faculty, the "discipline" model would appear to be the dominant driving force with respect to its organization, expectations, and rewards system. Some believe this is as it should be and would even strengthen the impact of this model – many members of the Faculty, especially those from departments which are primarily graduate in nature; most "discipline" faculties in the University; and the "academic" community of scholars. However, others believe that a substantial shift toward the "professional" model, especially with respect to organization, programming, and the rewards system, is necessary – many members of the Faculty, many "professional" faculties in the University, the education profession, and most practising systems. Much of the literature in the field and many of the recent developments in teacher education would also support a substantial shift toward the "professional" model.
>
> The impact of tradition and the inertia present in most large organizations could well influence the resolution of this issue as might the reduction in financial support. However, the primary factor in the resolution of the issue could well be the willingness of the Faculty, its leaders, and its members to take risks and act boldly.

An issue can be examined in terms of the conditions and problems which have influenced or could influence the situation being investigated. Issues, then, can be thought of as either *problems* or sets of related problems (often defined as *contingencies*) which contribute to the existing situation o which must be solved if the objectives of the project are to be satisfactorily achieved. Issues can also be thought of as *conditions* or sets of related conditions (often defined as *constraints*) which cannot be modified and which either contribute to the existing situation or must be taken into account in developing a set of circumstances which will lead to the satisfactory achievement of the objectives of the project.

If an issue is identified as a problem (contingency), the implication is that it can be solved in terms of the objectives of the project. However, if an issue is identified as a condition (constraint), the implication is that it cannot be modified appreciably, but it must be taken into account in the study conclusions and recommendations. For example, consider a team of engineers responsible for constructing a road between two towns along the shortest route. If they encounter a small stream, they would define this as a problem which is feasible to overcome without lengthening the route, simply by building a small bridge. However, if they encounter a large lake, they would define this as a constraint or condition which must be taken into account in building the road. It would probably not be feasible to build a bridge or a causeway; therefore, they must accept the condition and go around the lake, even though the length of the road is thereby extended.

Issues (of either the contingency or constraint variety) can be classified as internal or external to the situation or the organization involved. An issue is internal if decisions respecting it can be made by the involved organization. An issue is external if decisions respecting it must be made at least in part by some other organization.

Illustrative Issues

Appendix D contains elaborations of the issues identified in a particular project. Issues of both the problem (contingency) and condition (constraint) variety were identified in this study of the attendance area policies of the "Blue Mountain School Division" (all names in this excerpt have been changed).

Contingencies. Road conditions were identified as a problem (contingency) in relation to school attendance areas because it is feasible to modify them in the short term, to some degree at least. However, this issue was classified as an external problem because jurisdiction over the roads rested with the municipal authorities and not with the school jurisdiction. The present attendance area policies and practices in the school system were also identified as a contingency because it was possible to modify them. But this set of issues was classified as internal because its modification was under the control of the Board of Trustees.

Constraints. The socioeconomic conditions in the area were identified as an external constraint with respect to the purposes of the study. That is, any policy or program dealing with attendance areas had to take into account the socioeconomic conditions of the area. These conditions were not identified as a problem (contingency) because they could not be readily changed, nor were they classified as internal because they were not under the control of the school authorities. The location of school facilities was also identified as a constraint with respect to the development or modification of school attendance area policies, because school locations could not be readily changed, at least in the short term. However, the issue of school location was identified as an internal constraint because it was under the control of the school jurisdiction.

The difficulties of resolving an issue increase as it changes from a contingency to a constraint, and as control of its resolution moves from internal to external. For example, with respect to the Blue Mountain attendance area concerns, it would be easier to modify the attendance area policies than to modify the road conditions or the location of facilities, or to change the socioeconomic conditions in the area. This does not imply, however, that resolution of these latter issues should not be attempted.

Procedures in Issue Identification

To identify and elaborate issues, the researcher must synthesize and creatively interpret several sets of information:

1. The *rationale, purposes, and objectives* of the program being studied;
2. The *findings* of the study: all of the analyzed and interpreted data collected for the purposes of the project (e.g., literature review, document reviews, surveys, observations, etc.);
3. A variety of *models* drawn from the literature or created for the purposes of the study (see Chapter 4); and
4. The *knowledge and experience* of the researcher and of those working with the researcher.

When the researcher is identifying and elaborating issues, he or she must synthesize and interpret the above information in terms of the problems or constraints which have influenced or might influence the achievement of the intents of the policy area or program being investigated. Following the initial identification of problems and constraints, the researcher should attempt to coalesce them into major sets of issues. For example, the conditions concerning (a) barriers to transportation (deep valleys and rivers), (b) the agricultural economy, (c) sparse settlement, and (d) isolation from major urban centers – all of which might influence the policies and programs pertaining to attendance areas – can be synthesized into one issue dealing with the geographic and economic environments in which the school system operates.

Following initial identification and synthesis, the issues should be checked for appropriateness, accuracy and completeness. The researcher should ask the following questions.

1. Do the issues grow out of the findings of the study?

2. Are they truly problems and conditions which have influenced or can influence the direction or movement toward the objectives of the program being investigated?

3. Have I investigated all possible areas in which issues can occur?

The identification and verification of issues involves a complex set of functions which call for sophisticated skills in analysis and synthesis, as well as highly developed conceptual and interpersonal skills. Although the technical skills of communicating and analyzing can be of help, the tasks are basically conceptual and creative in nature. Therefore, the effectiveness of issue identification and verification can be increased if several knowledgeable people with a variety of backgrounds and expertise are involved in the process.

A judicious combination of individual assignments and group problem-solving procedures will probably bring out the most appropriate and accurate set of issues. For example, a number of people either involved in the project or knowledgeable about the situation or the substantive area of the study can hold a "brainstorming" session to develop an initial set of problems, conditions, and concerns. Adequate preparation for such a session is mandatory; those involved must become well versed about the project; they must have studied the findings; they must be informed about the definition of the term "issue" as it is used for the project; and they must be briefed on the procedures to be used in the brainstorming session. One or more individuals can then be assigned the task of synthesizing the products of such a session into sets of issues, verifying the issues against the study findings, and checking on appropriateness and completeness. Their ideas and conclusions can then be fed back to the brainstorming panel for reaction. Following this, the issue identification section of the report can be prepared.

Issue Elaboration

Three components should be included in the presentation of an issue First, the issue and its sub-components (problems and conditions) should be presented as clearly and concisely as possible. Second, to verify that the issue does in fact exist, illustrations of its presence in the situation should be presented. Third, the issue should be discussed in terms of its magnitude importance, and difficulty of resolution. If appropriate, the discussion should also include solutions to the problem or strategies for dealing with the condition. The following example illustrates one approach to the presentation of an issue. Appendix D illustrates another approach.

LEADERSHIP IN VOLUNTEER ORGANIZATIONS
ISSUE V

The Issue

A major set of problems faced by most volunteer organizations is the attraction of competent and motivated leadership personnel, the maintenance of this leadership over a sufficient period of time to have optimum impact, and the provision of leadership succession without seriously disrupting the organization. These problems are magnified in situations such as those faced in most societies where the pool of leadership potential is small because of the size of the communities, where several volunteer organizations are competing for the same pool of talent, and where the volunteer society has an unclear mandate and an uncertain future.

Illustrations

The leadership problem has manifested itself in different ways in different societies. However, most societies have had some problems. One society faced collapse when its leadership was lost through staff turnover in the school and the loss of a key member to another community. Another is facing serious difficulties because of succession problems – the leadership changed drastically because of conflict between two factions. Others have had to turn to the schools and other human resources professionals to help them out of difficulties in conducting meetings and administering the affairs of the society.

Discussion

All of the problems associated with leadership in volunteer organizations cannot be overcome; however, some steps might be taken to soften their impact on the operation of the societies. For example, as the societies become more stable and their mandates are clarified, it should be easier to attract and hold good leadership. It may also be possible to increase the pool of competent potential leaders by offering workshops and short courses for Board members on topics such as conducting meetings, managing conflict, problem solving, program planning, and communications.

In presenting and discussing an issue, the researcher should keep in mind that the "issues" section of a project provides the major backdrop for generating alternative directions and for developing any recommendations which may result from the project.

Alternative Generation and Feasibility Testing

Generating alternatives is an essential component of policy, development, and evaluation studies. It is necessary in each of these types of projects to know what the feasible alternatives are in order to arrive at defensible conclusions and recommend future courses of action. The nature of the alternatives generated will, of course, vary with the type of project. Generating and testing alternatives is the next logical step after the researcher interprets the data, formulates implications, and identifies issues.

Definition

An "alternative" can be defined as a policy, program, plan, or course of action which might resolve an identified issue or meet one or more purposes of a project. The term "alternative" implies that more than one policy, program, plan, or course of action is being considered. For example, in a study of attendance areas, several alternative policies were generated concerning the schools that elementary students could attend. These included the following:

1. Students may attend any school in the Division, with the Division providing transportation.

2. Although school attendance areas are established, students may attend any school in the system – if the decision is made by the preceding June 30 – with the Division providing transportation only if the routes exist and there is room on the buses.

3. Students must attend the school in their designated attendance area unless they are given special permission by the Board to attend another school.

The generation and consideration of more than one alternative is suggested for two reasons. First, it motivates the researchers to examine a broad spectrum of possibilities; second, it gives the decision makers a choice – other than a "yes" or "no." Some alternatives may not be acceptable to the stakeholders or decision makers concerned, and some may be more acceptable than others, based on the criteria selected to judge them. If there is a policy, program, or plan presently in place – as is usually the case – it should be considered as one of the alternatives. In fact, because of built-in resistance to change, present practice is generally a very strong alternative. For example, in the case of the alternative school attendance policies illustrated in Chapter 5, the third alternative (which was the existing policy) was finally chosen, even though the other alternatives were judged more desirable on the basis of the study findings.

The Alternative Generation Process

The alternative generation process requires a particular orientation on the part of the researchers, appropriate information, an alternative generation framework, and a set of procedures.

An Orientation

Generating alternatives requires researchers to adopt an orientation which assumes that there are no "right solutions" but, rather, a range of solutions, each with its own strengths and weaknesses. It also requires decision makers – all of whom have their own orientations and biases – to make a choice from among the alternatives. The role of the researcher is to identify or generate suitable alternatives and to test the feasibility of each, using a framework and a set of guidelines which take into account the purposes of the project, information gained from the study, knowledge in the field, and the economic, social, and political situation facing the decision makers.

Needed Information

Several sets of information are needed in order to identify and/or generate an appropriate set of alternatives. These include (a) the "findings" of the study and supporting documentation; (b) literature reviews in the area under study and reports on practices tried or considered in other jurisdictions (which could be considered as part of the study findings); and (c) the theoretical and conceptual models used for the study or developed for alternative generation.

Frameworks

A framework for alternative generation is similar to a conceptual model for guiding the overall study, and it serves a similar purpose. It is a model selected or designed specifically for the purpose of generating alternatives. The background concepts and knowledge necessary to develop an alternative generation framework come from the findings of and the experiences with the study, and from the related literature.

Figure 12 portrays a model designed to help in assigning alternative personnel policies to areas such as employment, assignment, working conditions, supervision and evaluation, staff development, and termination. Alternative policies were placed along a continuum from flexible to inflexible. This model served two purposes: to suggest areas in which alternative policies should be generated, and to assist in categorizing policy statements. Appendix E contains a framework designed to assist in developing alternative policies and programs which would encourage parents, teachers, and other community members in small, isolated northern communities to work together in planning and developing activities to better meet the educational needs of community members, especially school-aged children.

Procedures for Alternative Generation

There is no "right" set of procedures for alternative generation. The procedures must be governed by the type of project, as well as the style and preferences of the research team. However, the following steps and approaches to the process have proven useful in a number of policy and program development projects in which the author has been involved.

1. Select a team of knowledgeable people – people who will not let their own biases unduly affect their thinking – for the alternative generation panel. People knowledgeable about the situation being studied and its environment should be included, as should people knowledgeable about the disciplines and substantive areas involved.

2. Prior to the first assignment given to the alternative generation panel, provide panel members with all relevant documents: (a) the purposes, objectives, and design of the project; (b) the study findings and the supporting documents (e.g., data analysis and interpretation, document reviews, and literature reviews); (c) the models used in the study; and (d) the procedures to be used in alternative generation. It is advisable to have an orientation session with the panel, as everyone involved in the alternative generation process must be fully informed about the substance of the study and the processes being used.

Personnel Policy Area ＼ Alternative	Flexibility Flexible ◄──────────────► Inflexible			
Employment				
Assignment				
Working Conditions				
Supervision and Evaluation				
Staff Development				
Termination				

Figure 12

**Model for Assigning Alternatives to Each
Personnel Policy Area by Degree of Flexibility**

3. If you wish, assign each panel member the responsibility of generating ideas for alternatives in one or more of the areas under investigation. These need not and probably should not be "full-blown" alternatives.

4. Have one individual or a small sub-group from the alternative generation panel synthesize the ideas that have been generated.

5. Arrange a "brainstorming" session of the panel to consider and add to the synthesized set of ideas. To facilitate the conceptualization process, apply the following principles and practices usually associated with brainstorming: (a) prepare the panel members for the session by providing them with all background materials and with the purposes of the session, and by stressing the importance of a thorough knowledge of the materials prior to the session; (b) set the stage through an orientation session in which the processes to be used are discussed and a realistic backdrop is provided; (c) establish ground rules for the session – the most important ground rule is that no criticism is allowed (premature criticism thwarts the creative process). The only criterion for an idea is its relevance to the problem.

6. Following the brainstorming session, the ideas generated must be synthesized, summarized, and then fleshed out into full alternatives, perhaps

by a small sub-group from the panel. This process may include the addition of new ideas to fill in gaps, or the elimination of some which are obviously not feasible. Not all possible alternatives can be generated or presented; only the most appropriate should be included in the presentation.

7. Continue this process of panel consideration followed by individual or small group assignments until a satisfactory set of alternatives is arrived at. The alternatives generated should represent the full scope covered by the framework.

Testing the Feasibility of Alternatives

During the alternative generation process, some thought should be given to the feasibility of each alternative being considered so that only the alternatives which have some chance of success are included. However, in most situations it is desirable to take a closer look at the comparative feasibility of the alternatives generated. Therefore, after the most appropriate alternatives have been generated, they need to be compared on variables relevant to their desirability and feasibility.

Common Feasibility Variables

Four variables are probably appropriate to include in testing the feasibility of any alternative:

1. *Workability*: the extent to which the alternative will work, that is, solve the problem or meet the conditions required.
2. *Practicality*: the extent to which human and financial resources are available to implement the alternative.
3. *Acceptability*: the extent to which the decision makers and other stakeholders will accept the alternative.
4. *Diffusibility*: the ease with which the alternative can be communicated and disseminated.

Alternatives should also be tested for their compatibility with the objectives of the project and their usefulness in resolving the issues identified. Therefore, in addition to the four common variables outlined above, the following variables could be considered in the development of the feasibility test:

5. *Objectives*: the degree to which the alternative is compatible with the objectives of the study.
6. *Alternative Generation Framework, Guidelines, and Criteria*: the degree to which the alternative fits the framework, and any guidelines

and criteria established.

7. *Issues*: the extent to which the alternative helps in resolving the issues identified.

Other Feasibility Variables

Other variables unique to the alternatives being tested and to the context in which they are being tested may also be identified. For example, the following excerpt from a report on the evaluation of a four-day scheduling plan for a high school contains a set of guidelines for developing and testing alternative scheduling programs.

1. The scheduling system [must have] the potential for exceeding the minimum requirements established by the province.

2. The scheduling system must be educationally sound (e.g. facilitates learning, growth in maturity, teacher-student relationships, and self-direction).

3. The scheduling system must be compatible with the educational needs and learning styles of the various types of students in a community.

4. The scheduling system must be compatible with the educational philosophy of the system.

5. The scheduling system should enhance the development and maintenance of a school identity.

6. The scheduling system should facilitate the planning and the preparational and assessment tasks of teachers.

7. The scheduling system should be compatible with the expectations and the life styles represented in the community.

8. The scheduling system must be financially viable for the system.

9. The scheduling system must be administratively workable.

Some of these guidelines have to do with common feasibility variables such as acceptability and workability discussed above; others are unique to the study – for example, "The scheduling system has the potential for exceeding the minimum requirements established by the province" and "The scheduling system should enhance the development and maintenance of school identity."

In addition to a set of guidelines for developing and testing alternatives, criteria for applying the guidelines can also be useful. The following criteria were developed for the evaluation of the scheduling program described above.

1. A sound educational program is facilitated by a scheduling program which provides for blocks of optional time.

2. A sound educational program is enhanced if students are expected to plan and be responsible for learning activities during optional time blocks.

3. Varied opportunities to participate in educational activities increase the likelihood that students will benefit educationally from their use of optional time.

4. A teacher consultant program would assist students in making appropriate choices regarding use of optional time and would facilitate the maturing process.

Frameworks and criteria for their application could well be developed prior to alternative generation so that they can be applied to this process as well.

The Nature of the Feasibility Test

A feasibility testing process can be as simple as a one-hour session in which the general feasibility of each alternative is discussed on the basis of variables such as those outlined above, or it can be as complex as the development of a "paper and pencil" test which is administered to a panel of experts and discussed in a series of seminar sessions. For example, if the problem is to provide program development assistance to teachers, a test question under the "workability" category might read "Will the proposed program actually provide the teachers with assistance in evaluating and developing instructional programs?"

Various systems can be developed for applying the feasibility test. For example, a matrix with the test items divided into the appropriate sections on one axis, and the alternatives being considered on the other axis can be constructed (see Figure 13). Each alternative (A, B, C) on the horizontal axis can be rated on a five-point scale for each test item on the vertical axis. Each item can be weighted, again on a five-point scale, in relation to its importance in comparison with other items in the same section. The total of the weighted item scores for each alternative in each section is then divided by the number of items in the section. This gives an average item score for each alternative in each section of the test. Each section can also be weighted on a five-point scale to indicate its importance in relationship to the other sections of the test. The average item scores for each alternative in each section of the test can be multiplied by the weight factor for the section. This gives a score for each alternative in each section. The section scores for each alternative are then totalled to give the score on the feasibility test for each alternative.

Alternatives / Test Items	Weighting of Item	Weighting of Section	Ratings for Alternatives Low (1 High 5)					
			A		B		C	
			Rating	Score	Rating	Score	Rating	Score
Section I								
1............	1		1	1	3	3	5	5
2............	3	3	2	6	2	6	2	6
3............	2		5	10	3	6	2	4
4............	1		1	1	1	1	1	1
Total of item scores				18		16		16
Section Score [3 (Total ÷ 4)]			**13.5**		**12**		**12**	
Section II								
1............	1		2	2	3	3	1	1
2............	1		4	4	2	2	1	1
3............	4	4	3	12	5	20	2	8
4............	2		1	2	4	8	5	10
5............	1		2	2	2	2	2	2
6............	1		3	3	2	2	4	4
Total of item scores				25		37		26
Section Score [4 (Total ÷ 6)]			**16.8**		**24.8**		**17.2**	
Section III								
1............	1	6	3	3	1	1	5	5
2............	1		2	2	4	4	3	3
Total of item scores				5		5		8
Section Score [6 (Total ÷ 2)]			**15**		**15**		**24**	
TOTALS			**45.3**		**51.8**		**53.2**	

Figure 13

A Feasibility Testing Matrix

The individual or group responsible for applying the test may take different approaches to determining the rating for each item. A group may decide on a rating through discussion leading to a consensus, or the group may conduct a discussion followed by individual ratings which are averaged to produce the group rating. Whichever method is used, as much information as possible should be gathered and considered. The test does not have to be completed in one sitting: if the group is considering a particular item and decides that more information is needed, further consideration of the item may be delayed until the information is available.

The nature of the test will depend upon several factors: the magnitude of the risk involved in adopting any particular alternative, the nature of the study, and the orientation of the researchers. At minimum, the feasibility testing process should include (a) the selection of variables to be examined; (b) the identification of criteria for each feasibility variable; (c) the application of these criteria by at least one person to each alternative; and (d) a comparison of the alternatives being considered.

The following is a feasibility test of alternative personnel policies for a school system.

Alternative Personnel Policies
Rating Scale

1. **Potential**		*Of No Benefit*		*Highly Beneficial*		*Don't Know*
a) The implementation of this alternative will be of benefit to:						
1. Communities and their representatives	(4)	1	2	3	4	9
2. School administrators and teachers	(5)	1	2	3	4	9
3. Students	(6)	1	2	3	4	9
4. System-wide administrators	(7)	1	2	3	4	9

		Many Negative Effects		*No Negative Effects*		*Don't Know*
b) The implementation of this alternative will have negative effects on:						
1. Communities and their representatives	(8)	1	2	3	4	9
2. School administrators and teachers	(9)	1	2	3	4	9
3. Students	(10)	1	2	3	4	9
4. System-wide administrators	(11)	1	2	3	4	9
c) The benefit(s) will be of sufficient value to make the implementation of the alternative worthwhile.	(12)	1	2	3	4	9

2. Practicality		*Strongly Disagree*		*Strongly Agree*		*Don't Know*
a) In terms of human costs (that is, the impact on the people involved) the alternative is acceptable for:						
1. Communities and their representatives	(13)	1	2	3	4	9
2. School administrators and teachers	(14)	1	2	3	4	9
3. Students	(15)	1	2	3	4	9
4. System-wide administrators	(16)	1	2	3	4	9
b) The potential benefits justify the dollar costs involved in implementing this alternative.	(17)	1	2	3	4	9
c) The human resources required for the implementation of this alternative are available or obtainable.	(18)	1	2	3	4	9
d) The alternative is sufficiently described and understood for implementation.	(19)	1	2	3	4	9

3. Reliability

		Strongly Disagree		*Strongly Agree*		*Don't Know*
a) The alternative is able to "cope" with changes in the administrative situation.	(20)	1	2	3	4	9
b) The alternative will operate reliably; it will "stand up" over time.	(21)	1	2	3	4	9

4. Diffusibility

		Strongly Disagree		*Strongly Agree*		*Don't Know*
a) The alternative is compatible with the attitudes and values of:						
1. Communities and their representatives	(22)	1	2	3	4	9
2. School administrators and teachers	(23)	1	2	3	4	9
3. Students	(24)	1	2	3	4	9
4. System-wide administrators	(25)	1	2	3	4	9
b) The results from the implementation of this alternative can be demonstrated easily and convincingly.	(26)	1	2	3	4	9
c) The alternative can be adequately "packaged" for public relations purposes.	(27)	1	2	3	4	9
d) The alternative can be tried out on a limited basis before being fully implemented.	(28)	1	2	3	4	9

5. Tolerance The alternative is able to "cope" with:		*Strongly Disagree*		*Strongly Agree*		*Don't Know*
a) a sudden increase in enrolments	(29)	1	2	3	4	9
b) a gradual increase in enrolments	(30)	1	2	3	4	9
c) a sudden decrease in enrolments	(31)	1	2	3	4	9
d) a gradual decrease in enrolments	(32)	1	2	3	4	9
e) a geographical shift in enrolments	(33)	1	2	3	4	9

Procedures for Developing a Feasibility Test

Whichever approach to alternative testing is taken, the following set of procedures can facilitate the process:

1. Decide on the variables to be used in the feasibility test (e.g., from among those suggested above).

2. Develop test items and/or criteria for each variable. These may be simple questions to ask at a feasibility testing seminar, or they may be a complex set of questions for inclusion in a paper and pencil test such as the one presented above.

3. Determine the format and weightings for items and sections. Decisions need to be made concerning the scale or nature of the judgments made. For example, is a numerical scale to be used (1 to 5), or is the alternative to be judged on a "high-medium-low" scale? Some questions and some variables may be more important than others with respect to the overall feasibility of the alternative. This can be taken into account through applying weightings (see Figure 13).

4. Work out the procedures for administering the test. For example, is it to be a paper and pencil test completed individually by members of a testing panel, or one conducted openly by a group of people in a testing seminar?

5. Decide on who is to be involved in the test – for example, the research team, or a panel of experts, or a random sample of those affected?

The people selected to participate in the feasibility test must be well prepared. They must be knowledgeable about the findings of the study, the literature and practice in the field, and the situation in which the study is being conducted. If a panel is to be involved in the testing process, procedures similar to those suggested for alternative generation might well be considered.

Test Outcomes

The feasibility test, regardless of the approach taken, should allow the researchers to make defensible comments about the comparative feasibility of the alternatives being considered on a set of appropriate variables.

8

Developing
Recommendations

The project proposal or specifications will probably indicate whether or not recommendations are called for. If the project purposes and design include the identification of issues and the generation and testing of alternatives, then substantive recommendations (a recommendation that one of the alternatives be accepted) are generally not necessary. The presentation and discussion of the various alternatives should provide sufficient information for the contracting agency to proceed with the decision-making process. If recommendations are not included, the contracting agency is forced to consider the various alternatives carefully and then make a decision – this is as it should be. However, if substantive recommendations are to be included, the following suggestions may be useful.

Substantive Recommendations

The recommendations made should follow from the objectives of the study and should be based on the study findings, the issues identified, and the results of the feasibility test of the alternatives generated. The presentation of each recommendation should make it obvious to the reader that the recommendation is based upon the results of the study and not upon the beliefs and biases of the researcher. Therefore, the presentation of the recommendations should include (a) the alternative being recommended; (b) the reason for making the recommendation (results of the feasibility test); (c) the implications of the recommendation; and (d) the second and third choices, if appropriate (it is generally desirable to leave room for discretionary choice).

The nature and design of the project will determine in large measure how and where the recommendations appear in the report. In most cases they will be included along with the feasibility test of the alternatives, or as a conclusion to the alternatives section. In some cases, however, they may be presented in a separate section or chapter. The following is an extract from a report on a study of attendance areas in a school division in which the recommendations were presented in a separate chapter. Only one of several recommendations is included, though they all followed the same format.

Recommendations

Specific recommendations in respect to policies, regulations, and programs will not be made in this report. These are matters for the Board and its officials to determine. However, recommendations respecting "orientation to action" based on the literature reviewed, practices in the Province and elsewhere, the situation in the Division, and the findings of the study will be presented for the consideration of the Board. A process for considering the report and for implementing the recommendations selected is also suggested.

Quality Education

The variations in communities, the isolation of some communities, the variations in school size, and the overall differences in orientations of the people in the region would suggest that the Quality Based on Student Needs and Cultural Perspectives alternative would be the most appropriate for the Division. Although on first consideration this alternative may seem impossible, too costly, and a placation to the malcontents and complainers, it is probably the alternative which would best meet the long-term needs of the people of the area. This orientation favors the development of programs and delivery mechanisms which would best meet the needs and wants of a wide variety of interest groups and people who hold different philosophical positions.

The success of this orientation would depend on the commitment of the Board and its staff. In the short term, priority would have to be given to developing and testing appropriate innovative programs and delivery mechanisms. Many such programs exist, and others could be developed. Although funding support for developing such programs is more difficult to get than it was a few years ago, funds are still available. The process of converting to this orientation would be slow. It would involve much planning and community involvement, and many innovative pilot projects would be necessary. However, this period of "changeover" would be both exciting and rewarding.

The following extract from a report on a project concerning the development of a continuing education system is an example of how recommendations can be incorporated into the discussion of the feasibility of alternatives.

Application of the Framework
to Continuing Education in the Region

A wide range of alternative program, delivery, governance, and finance systems could be developed for a continuing education enterprise by considering all of the possible answers to the questions posed in the framework. In fact, the range would be so wide and varied that it would be of little use in making concrete policy decisions. Therefore, in order to focus on more feasible alternatives, it was necessary to apply evaluative guidelines to the alternatives.

The application of these guidelines in considering the questions in the framework produced an "orientation to action" which was used in making policy recommendations for establishing operational plans. The following recommendations should serve in the promulgation of general policy, not in establishing plans for specific structures and programs. Operational plans must be developed after policy recommendations have been established.

Program

The questions posed under the program dimensions of the framework were approached by considering alternative positions along continua such as degree of openness, flexibility, comprehensiveness, breadth, and adaptability. Application of the guidelines assisted in selecting the most appropriate position in each separate continuum.

Question 1: Who should be served by the continuing education system?
The first guideline stressed that all adult residents should have equal educational opportunities. Therefore, all adults should have access to some continuing education programs. However, because of present variations in need, resources, and opportunities it may be necessary to provide incentives to special groups (for example, natives, those outside of the capital city, those requiring vocational preparation, and those requiring academic upgrading and life-skills). Because of these conditions which change over time, a flexible adaptable approach to selecting clients for special emphasis needs to be taken.

In order to smooth the transition from elementary and secondary education to continuing education, the term "adult" should be defined broadly to include any person sixteen years of age or over who has left high school, or who is recommended for admission by a school principal.

In general, the orientation to action in respect to the clients to be served should be "openness" and "flexibility."

DEGREE OF OPENNESS AND FLEXIBILITY

Low   High

1. That programs be designed to serve the needs of adults gen-
    erally and that no restrictions in the form of lower age lim-
    its for students be imposed.

Process Recommendations

The planning and policy-making processes are often as critical as the
substantive recommendations (if not more critical). Therefore, it is generally
desirable to recommend a set of processes for considering the report, making decisions, and implementing the alternatives selected. The following
extract from the report on the aforementioned attendance area study is an
example of the type of process recommendations which can be useful.

Suggestions for Considering the Report and Implementing Decisions

It is recommended that this report be given wide distribution throughout
the Division and that procedures for its consideration be established and
well publicized. Procedures such as the following are suggested:

(a) An overall planning committee consisting of representatives from the
Board, the Superintendent of Schools, principals, teachers, students, and
parents could be established to oversee the consideration process and
prepare a final report including recommendations for the Board. To be
effective, this committee should have no more than twelve members.

(b) The Planning Committee could establish a set of task forces to study
and make recommendations on the various areas contained in this report.
Each task force should have on its membership a wide representation of
people who are interested and competent in the area under consideration.
No task force should have more than eight or ten members. Terms of
reference for the task forces should be clear and deadlines for reporting
should be set.

(c) Hearings before the Planning Committee should be held and briefs
requested and welcomed. This procedure would ensure opportunities for
broad involvement which would be necessary for the success of the operation.

(d) Although most of the work should be done by local people, it may be desirable to involve external consultants from time to time.

(e) If possible the Board should place a moratorium on decisions relevant to the issues raised in this report until the Planning Committee has completed its work and made its recommendations.

(f) The development and implementation of the specific policies and programs growing out of the work of the Planning Committee should be done slowly and primarily through the project mode of operation.

9

Reporting

There are two types of reporting requirements in any project: progress reporting and final reporting.

Progress Reporting

It is always desirable (and generally a requirement of the contract) to make progress reports at various stages during the conduct of a project. A progress report provides feedback for decision making by the policy or steering committee and the researchers. It also keeps the principals informed about and involved in the project.

A progress report usually contains two sections: a *procedural* report on the project activities and plans, and a *substantive* report on the tentative findings, issues, alternatives, or recommendations. A general rule of thumb is to present a brief, written procedural report and to present any substantive reports orally with the aid of charts, overhead transparencies, or other audio-visual aids. Written substantive reports take more time to prepare and can lock the researchers into decisions or positions too early in the life of the project. Written substantive reports, even if they are tentative in nature, can also be interpreted by the principals and other stakeholders as the final position. This is especially so if they are distributed – as they usually are – to interested parties who were not present at the reporting session. If written substantive reports are necessary in order to elicit the type of feedback which cannot be obtained at a reporting session, care must be taken to ensure that those reading the report realize that the information is tentative in nature and is presented only for the purpose of eliciting reactions.

Progress reports should be made up of the following: (a) the initial design for the conduct of the project; (b) the specific design for data collection and analysis; (c) completion of the findings; (d) identification of the issues; and (e) completion of the alternatives and the feasibility test.

For purposes of illustration, extracts from the first progress report to the Steering Committee for the Education North Evaluation Project are con tained in Appendix F.

Final Reporting

The primary purpose of the final report is to provide the best and mos usable information possible, under the terms of the project purposes an objectives, to the principals and other stakeholder groups. A secondary pur pose for most researchers, especially if they are members of a university faculty, is to add to the fund of knowledge in the field.

In designing and preparing the final report there are five factors to con sider: technical quality, communicability, conservation of the reader's time credibility, and replicability.

Technical Quality

The report should be presented in an acceptable and attractive style an format (headings and sub-headings, footnotes and references, figures, tables charts, presentation style, spacing, print, binding, cover, etc.). Many organi zations have policies or practices pertaining to the style and format c reports. Any requirements in this regard should be investigated before deci sions are made. If style and format are not governed by policies, then som acceptable style which best fits the purpose and nature of the report shoul be selected. Campbell, Ballou, and Slade (1986) is a good general referenc for style and format. Accuracy in sentence construction, grammar, spelling and punctuation is also essential.

Communicability

The most important characteristic of the report is that it communicate to the target audiences what the researchers want to communicate. Th report should be prepared primarily for the major target audience. If th major audience is school board members, then the report might be in a di ferent style than it would be if the major audience were made up of academ ics in a university. However, care must also be taken to communicate to a stakeholder audiences. The sequencing of information is important, as ease of reading and clarity of expression. Illustrative Tables of Contents ar provided in Appendix G. Emphasis on the key features of the study is vit – purposes, design, findings, issues, alternatives, and recommendation Most readers want to know the purpose and conclusions of the study befor they go through the detailed findings and procedures.

Conservation of Reader Time

The major audience of most policy, evaluation, and program development reports is composed of busy people who want to get at the issues and recommendations as quickly as possible. Therefore, it is the responsibility of the researchers to prepare and sequence the report to meet this need, while still maintaining their integrity as researchers. One effective way of doing this is through an executive summary which presents the essence of the report in a few pages, generally not over ten. In some cases it is best to present the executive summary in chronological sequence – rationale, purpose, objectives, findings, issues, alternatives, and recommendations. This is usually necessary if an understanding of the recommendations requires knowledge of how the project was conducted and what the findings were. In other cases it is best to present the purposes and then the recommendations, followed by the findings, issues, alternatives, and design.

The report itself should be organized carefully to present a logical flow of information and an understanding of how one section leads out of the previous one. Only the data and supporting documentation necessary for understanding the findings and their interpretation should be contained in the report itself. The data and supporting documentation necessary to confirm the findings and interpretations should be included in appendices and/or technical documents. Technical documents may accompany the report, or they may be available in the offices of the researcher and the contracting agency.

Numerical data are often best presented in a set of tables, each capable of being understood and interpreted without the accompanying text. The text should also be understandable without the accompanying tables; however, it should not merely constitute a presentation of the same information in textual form. The text should draw attention to the most important information contained in the tables and then discuss and interpret this information.

Researcher Credibility

The credibility of the report and of the researchers depends in large measure on the acceptance by the principals and the research community of the methods used (objectives, research questions, data sources, sampling techniques, data-collecting instruments and devices, methods of analysis, procedures for interpretation and presentation of findings, procedures for issue identification and alternative generation and testing). Therefore, methods acceptable to both should be selected and scrupulously applied.

These methods should be reported and defended in summary form in the report and if necessary elaborated in the appendices. The report should also clearly demonstrate that the conclusions and recommendations flow from the data – including the literature – and not from the biases of the researcher or any one interest group.

Replicability

Other researchers or practitioners may wish to replicate the study either for research purposes or for problem solution. Therefore, all information necessary for replication should be contained in the report and its appendices or in available technical documents. Most of this information is also necessary to establish credibility, as discussed above. The methods of instrument development, sample selection, data collection, data analysis and interpretation, and procedures for issue identification, alternative development and testing, and recommendation development should be reported in sufficient detail so that others are able to replicate the study. The support for and defence of these procedures should also be included.

Presentation of the Report

Once the report is in a form acceptable to the researchers, it is advisable to present it as a preliminary report to the policy or steering committee for reaction. This provides an opportunity for correction of errors and misunderstandings, and for reactions to its style, format, and contents. The reactions of the steering committee should be considered but not necessarily included in the final report to the principals.

References

Beishon, J., & Peters, G. (Eds.). (1976). *System behavior.* New York, NY: Harper & Row.

Bennis, W. (1983). The art of leadership. In Suresh Srivastva & Associates (Eds.), *The executive mind* (pp. 15-24). San Francisco, CA: Jossey-Bass.

Bennis, W., & Nanus, B. (1985). *Leaders, the strategies for taking charge.* New York, NY: Harper & Row.

Bogdan, R.C., & Biklen, S.K. (1982). *Qualitative research for education: An introduction to theory and methods.* Boston, MA: Allyn Bacon.

Borg, W.R., & Gall, M.D. (1983). *Educational research: An introduction* (4th ed.). New York, NY: Longman.

Borich, G.D., & Jemelka, R.R. (1982). *Programs and systems: An evaluation perspective.* New York, NY: Academic Press.

Bradburn, N.M., Sudman, S., & Associates. (1979). *Improving interview methods and questionnaire design: Response effects to threatening questions in survey research.* San Francisco, CA: Jossey-Bass.

Campbell, W.G., Ballou, S.V., & Slade, C. (1986). *Form and style: Theses, reports, term papers* (7th ed.). Boston, MA: Houghton-Mifflin.

Downey, L.W. (1976). *The school superintendency in 1976.* A report prepared for the Alberta Department of Education. Edmonton, AB: L.W. Downey Research Associates.

Erickson, B.H., & Nosanchuk, T.A. (1977). *Understanding data.* Toronto, ON: McGraw-Hill Ryerson.

Federal Statistical Activities Secretariat. (1979). *Basic questionnaire design* (2nd ed.). Ottawa, ON: Statistics Canada.

Ferguson, G.A. (1976). *Statistical analysis in psychology and education* (4th ed.). New York, NY: McGraw-Hill.

Ingram, E.J. (1984). *Design for a review development project.* A report prepared for the Strathcona County Board of Education.

Ingram, E.J., & McIntosh, R.G. (1983). *Building school-community relationships in the north: A sourcebook of policy alternatives.* Edmonton, AB: Alberta Education.

Ingram, E.J., & McIntosh, R.G. (1983). *Education North evaluation project: Final report.* Edmonton, AB: Alberta Education.

Kerlinger, F.N. (1979). *Behavioral research: A conceptual approach.* New York, NY: Holt, Rinehart & Winston.

81

Kidder, L.H. (1981). *Research methods in social relations.* (4th ed.). New York, NY: Holt, Rinehart & Winston.

McNeil, D.R. (1977). *Interactive data analysis: A practical primer.* New York, NY: John Wiley & Sons.

Miklos, E. (1975). *Approaches to school administration.* A paper prepared for the Education Division of the Commonwealth Secretariat.

Miklos, E., Ingram, E.J., & McIntosh, R.G. (1971). *Planning for educational development.* A report prepared for the Yellowhead School Division.

Orlich, D.C. (1978). *Designing sensible surveys.* Pleasantville, NY: Redgrave.

Osborn, R.N., Morris, F.A., & Conner, P.E. (1984). Emerging technologies: The challenge to leadership theory. In J.G. Hunt, D-M. Hosking, C.A. Schriesheim, & R. Stewart (Eds.), *Leaders and managers: International perspectives on management behavior and leadership* (pp. 360-365). New York, NY: Pergamon.

Selye, H.A. (1974). *Stress without distress.* Toronto, ON: McClelland & Stewart.

Simon, A., & Boyer, E.G. (Eds.). (1970). *Mirrors for behaviour II: An anthology of observation instruments.* Philadelphia, PA: Research for Better Schools.

Stake, R. E. (1967). The countenance of educational evaluation. *Teachers College Record, 68,* 523-540.

Sudman, S., & Bradburn, N.M. (1983). *Asking questions: A practical guide to questionnaire design.* San Francisco, CA: Jossey-Bass.

van Gigch, J.P. (1978). *Applied general systems theory.* New York: Harper & Row

von Bertalanffy, L. (1968). *General system theory.* New York, NY: Braziller.

Appendix A

Requests for Proposals

Requests for Proposals
from the
Department of Advanced Education

The enclosed RFPs have been originated by the Department of
Advanced Education.

The foundation of planning and policy development implies access to a
body of information which is organized in a manner consistent with certain
specified planning issues.

The Department has gathered and is gathering and analyzing information concerning the province's population and economic status. This information is made useful by its transformation and application in decision-
making at both policy and program levels. Currently, a need exists to organ-
ize population and economic information into an institutional region perspective. That is to say, the project will result in a number of proposals. In
turn, each of these proposals will serve as the terms of reference for a report
by each institutional region. These reports will outline the demographic
characteristics and the economic characteristics of the region. The following information should be of use in drafting the proposal.

The proposal should contain:

1. title
2. purpose of project – rationale
3. objectives and expected outcomes
4. methodology to be employed. (This can be somewhat general but
   should include details of the overall design – i.e., definition of institutional region, data elements required, etc.)
5. time line for the project
6. budget for the project, including manpower and other resource
   requirements
7. additional information as deemed necessary.

The activities outlined in the proposal should be described in such a
manner that they could be accomplished on either a contract or in-house
basis.

The overall time frame for having the projects undertaken and com
pleted is fiscal 1987-1988. The overall budget for each project is not t
exceed $50,000. During the conduct of these projects several sources c
existing information will be accessed. These sources, including many on fil
with the Department, will be made available during the development of th
proposal.

Request for Proposals: Project I

Project Title: Demographic Mapping of Institutional Service Regions
Purpose: To develop a demographic information package for each institutional region. The package would include information concerning:

1. population structure
   - numbers
   - age ranges
   - sex distribution
   - educational level
   - labor force skill levels
   - etc.
2. migration information
   - numbers – in and out
   - primary sources
   - age, sex, educational levels
   - etc.
3. forecasts of population change in Alberta to 2001.

Outcome: – A proposal to develop the demographic map in a consistent manner for the province but on a regional basis as defined by primary institutional service regions.

– Proposal to contain the methodology for completing the initial map and for updating the information on a yearly basis.

This information will be used by departmental and institutional officials in developing medium and long term plans.

Request for Proposals: Project II

Project Title: Economic Mapping of Institutional Service Regions

Purpose: To develop an economic information package for each institu
tional service region. The package would contain information
concerning:

1. major economic activities in region
   - primary sector
   - secondary sector
   - tertiary sector
2. labor force information
   - cyclical and seasonal shifts
   - employment/unemployment
   - shifts in labor force
3. forecasted developments
   - industrial growth
   - labor force growth

Outcome: - A proposal to develop the economic map in a consistent
manner for the province but on a regional basis as defined
by the primary institutional service regions.

- Proposal to contain the methodology for completing the
initial map and for updating the information on a quarterly
and/or yearly basis.

This information will be used by departmental and institutional officials in
developing medium and long term plans.

Appendix B

Project Proposals

School Administration in Transition

Canada, along with most other industrialized nations in the world, is witnessing a period of traumatic adjustment brought on by what some would call the emergence of the "post-industrial," or the "information" society. Naisbitt[1] has identified several trends in this emerging society: (1) a focus on the rapid processing, storage, and transmission of information; (2) a melding of a "high tech" and "high touch" working environment; (3) a move from numerous national economies to a world economy; (4) a shift from a short-term to a long-term planning focus; (5) a growth in self-help organizations and orientations; (6) a move from centralization to decentralization of control; (7) a shift from representative to participatory democracy; and (8) a move from hierarchies in the administration of organizations to a network mode of operation.

The initial reaction of most people and organizations to rapidly changing environments and technologies (such as the world has been experiencing over the past few years) is first to ignore them, then to use the new technologies to prop up the old structures while still resisting major changes, and then finally, but begrudgingly, to apply the new technologies and knowledge to adjust structures and modes of operation to bring them into harmony with the new environments.

The educational system is going through the same traumatic adjustments – and with the same reactions – as are most other segments of organized society. Initiatives in one segment of the system are often at variance with initiatives in another segment, or at least the two sets of initiatives are out of step; some elements of the system cling tenaciously to the past, whereas others race headlong into an uncharted future; strong differences exist among the parts of the system with respect to both ends and the means; and, as might be expected, the channels of communications among the parts of the system are confused and often clogged.

One way out of this morass is to look for common elements of concern and then for common approaches to bringing these particular elements of the system into line with the new technologies and the new environmental conditions. A major element in the educational system of this province which seems to be of concern to all stakeholders is the governance and administration of education at all levels. The school trustees' association has spearheaded a renewed interest in the role of the school principal and in the preparation and upgrading of educational administrators; the Department of Education has implemented a program which introduces a modified approach to the governance and administration of education in the Province, and the Department of Education and the school trustees' association are jointly funding a project to pull together and disseminate new approaches to educational management for the Province. The school superintendents' association and the teachers' association have also taken renewed interest in the administration of the educational system.

Although there are differences of opinions and different approaches being expressed regarding the administration of the system, there is at least a common area of concern and a common realization that administration is a key component of the system and that something must be done to rationalize and bring order to this component of the system. Therefore, a serious examination and, if necessary, reconceptualization of the administrative component of the educational system would be one appropriate starting point for moving the Province's educational system into harmony with the emerging information society. An appropriate starting point for initiatives by the administrators' council of the teachers' association would be "administration at the school level."

Purposes of the Study

It is proposed that the administrators' council of the teachers' association, in collaboration with the school superintendents' association, the school trustees' association, the Department of Educational Administration of the University and the Department of Education undertake a study of the administration of education in the Province at the school level. The major purpose of such a study would be to determine the current status in respect to provincial and local policies governing, and practices of, school administration; to identify those policies and practices which need to be modified in order to satisfy changing needs and conditions; to identify the issues surrounding the renewal of the practice of educational administration in the Province; to generate and test alternative policies and practices designed to close the gap between present policies and practices and the identified needs; and to consider ways and means of determining appropriate alternatives and moving toward their implementation. The study would include but not necessarily be limited to (1) a status study of administration at the school level (i.e., demographics, policies, structures, roles, tasks, selection, preparation, evaluation, orientations and relationships); (2) trends in school administration in the Province and elsewhere (i.e., policies, structures, roles, tasks, selection, preparation, evaluation, orientations and relationships); (3) projections respecting wants, needs and conditions affecting the administration of schools over the next ten years; (4) identification of issues facing the

system and administrators in respect to gaps between present policies and
practice and identified trends and needs (i.e., administrative structures, roles
and relationships; orientations to administration; administrative styles; the
preparation for administrative roles; the selection and evaluation of administrators; membership of administrators in professional organizations; and the
interface among the various levels of governance and administration); (5)
the generation of alternative policies and practices for meeting changing
needs and conditions; and (6) the generation of alternative approaches to the
renewal of school administration.

The emphasis of the project will be upon identifying gaps between
present policies and practices and changing needs and conditions, and identifying alternative approaches to narrowing these gaps.

Project Objectives

The objectives of the study team are as follows:

1. to determine the current status of school administration in the Province in respect to factors such as policies governing school administration;
structures for administering schools; roles of school administrators; tasks
carried out in the administration of schools; the preparation, selection and
evaluation of school administrators; orientations taken by school administrators toward their job; relationships of school administrators with teachers,
students, parents, the community, central office and the board; and the satis-
faction of school administrators with their job and their environment;

2. to determine the trends and needs in school administration in the
Province and elsewhere in respect to the factors listed in Objective 1;

3. to identify the factors (orientations, attitudes, policies, wants, needs,
knowledge and conditions) which could influence developments in school
administration over the next ten years;

4. to analyze, compare and interpret the data collected for Objectives 1
to 3 in terms of the purposes of the study;

5. to identify the issues facing the educational system in the Province
in respect to closing the gap between present policies and practices and
changing needs and conditions (i.e., orientations to administration; administrative structures, roles and relationships; administrative styles; the preparation, selection and evaluation of school administrators; the interface of
school administrators with the board and other levels of administration; the
membership of school administrators in professional organizations; and the
need for school administrators);

6. to generate alternative policies and practices for closing the gap between the present status and changing needs and conditions, to generate alternative approaches to the resolution of the issues identified in Objective 5, and to test the feasibility of each alternative; and

7. to report the findings of the study to the Project Steering Committee and to the administrators' council of the teachers' association.

Project Management

The project will be contracted to the Department of Educational Administration of the Provincial University. Dr. S. M. Timmons of the Department of Educational Administration will act as Project Director. He will be assisted by several other staff members and graduate students from the Department of Educational Administration. The project will be supervised by a Steering Committee made up of three members appointed by the administrators' council, a representative named by the teachers' association, and one member appointed by each of the collaborating organizations.

The study team will report to the Steering Committee following (1) the completion of the design for data collection and analysis; (2) the various stages of data analysis; (3) the preparation of the findings; (4) the identification of the issues; (5) the generation of alternative policies and practices and alternative approaches to issue resolution; (6) the preparation of the draft reports; and (7) the preparation of the final report.

Proposed Design

It is neither possible nor appropriate to develop the complete and final design of a project such as the one being proposed prior to the commencement of the project. A model(s) will be selected to assist in data collection, analysis and interpretation. The selection will be made following a review of available and appropriate models. The various Educational Management (Administration) models used by those involved in recent studies and projects in Province, including members from the staff of the Department of Education, will be given due consideration.

The following procedures will probably be used as the overall approach to conducting the study:

1. Data Collection
   - questionnaires and opinionnaires (all provincial principals and school superintendents and a sample of assistant principals, trustees,

teachers, parents, students, and other stakeholders)
- interviews with samples of the same groups to be surveyed by questionnaire plus other experts in the discipline, or related disciplines (no more than 150 in total)
- documents (demographics, policies, structures, studies, etc.) from a sample of provincial school systems and from elsewhere
- literature reviews
- case studies (observations, interviews, documents).

2. Data Analysis and Interpretation
- Each of the sets of data suggested above will be analyzed and appropriate comparisons and interpretations made. The analyzed data from some, or all, of the datasets (i.e., opinionnaires, demographics, literature) might be presented to regional conferences – or to other gatherings of stakeholders – as one device for interpreting and gathering reactions to the findings.
- The findings of the study will be synthesized and prepared (i.e., the status of school administration in Alberta, trends and changing conditions in school administration in Alberta and elsewhere, theory and research respecting school administration, projected needs in respect to the administration of schools, and a comparison and interpretation of the findings).

3. Issue Identification
- An issue is defined as a set of problems or conditions which must be resolved or taken into account in order to move effectively and efficiently toward the objectives of a program.
- Issue identification panels (i.e., the study team, representatives from stakeholder groups, experts) will be created and instructed in the application of the issue identification model and procedures adopted for this study.
- The issues identified will be presented to the Steering Committee and, if possible, to regional conferences for reaction.

4. Alternative Policies and Practices and Approaches to Issue Resolution
- alternative development panels (i.e., the study team, experts, representatives from stakeholder groups) will be created to assist in the generation and feasibility testing of various alternative policies and practices designed to close the gap between the present status and changing needs and conditions, and approaches to resolving the

issues identified in the study.
  - The alternatives generated will be presented to the Steering Committee and, if possible, to regional conferences for reaction.
5. Reporting
  - Progress reports will be presented to the Steering Committee and, if appropriate and possible, to regional conferences and other forums.
  - The final written report will be presented to the Steering Committee.
  - Other reporting models as agreed to by the Steering Committee and the study team will also be employed.

Phasing and Timing

The study will be conducted in six overlapping phases: (1) study design, (2) data collection, (3) data analysis and interpretation, (4) issue identification, (5) alternative generation and testing, and (6) reporting. Figure 1 depicts the overlapping nature of these phases and the time estimated to conduct each phase and the total project. It is proposed that the project begin by April 1, 1986, and that it be completed by April 30, 1988.

Budget Estimates

The manpower estimates are contained in Table 1. The total estimated costs of conducting the project are contained in Table 2. Table 3 contains the total cost estimates, the contributions which the Department of Educational Administration is prepared to make to the project, estimated contributions from other stakeholders and the price for which the Department of Educational Administration is prepared to contract the project. The Department of Educational Administration is prepared to contract the project for a total of $37 200.

---

[1]Naisbitt, *Megatrends: Ten new directions transforming our lives* (New York: Warner, 1982).

Table 1
Manpower Estimates by Phase

Phase	Manpower Category	Man-days
1. Design	Senior Researchers	20
	Junior Researchers	33
	Steering Committee	7
	Secretarial	15
2. Data Collection	Senior Researchers	53
	Junior Researchers	70
	Steering Committee	7
	Secretarial	10
3. Data Analysis	Senior Researchers	30
	Junior Researchers	30
	Steering Committee	7
	Secretarial	15
4. Issue Identification	Senior Researchers	15
	Junior Reseachers	15
	Steering Committee	3
	Secretarial	5
5. Alternative Generation	Senior Researchers	20
	Junior Researchers	20
	Steering Committee	3
	Secretarial	5
6. Reporting	Senior Researchers	30
	Junior Researchers	30
	Steering Committee	7
	Secretarial	30

Table 2
Budget Estimates by Phase

	1 Design	2 Data C	3 Analysis	4 Issues	5 Alt.	6 Report
Personnel						
Sr. Researchers	$6 000	$15 000	$9 000	$4 500	$6 000	$9 000
Jr. Researchers	4 950	10 500	4 500	2 250	3 000	4 500
Steering Comm.	2 100	2 100	2 100	900	900	2 100
Secretarial	900	600	900	300	300	1 800
	13 950	29 100	16 500	7 950	10 200	17 400
Project Total						95 100
Supplies/Printing/ Mailing	200	5 000	200	200	200	1 000
Project Total						6 800
Computer	100		2 000			500
Project total						2 600
Travel/Subsistence	300	1 000	500	500	500	300
Project Total						3 100
Phase Totals	$14 550	$35 100	$19 200	$8 650	$10 900	$19 200

Estimated Budget for Project
$107 600

Table 3
Budget Sharing

Budget Item	Total	Dept/Cont.	Other/Cont.	Contract
Personnel	$95 100	$52 100[1]	$10 200[2]	$32 800[3]
Supplies/Printing/ Mailing	6 800	1 000	4 800[4]	1 000
Computer	2 600	1 300[5]		1 300
Travel/Subsistence	3 100		1 000[6]	2 100
Total	$107 600	$54 400	$16 000	$37 200

[1]This contribution of the Department of Educational Administration includes the contribution of all Junior Researchers ($29 700), the salary paid to staff for instructional purposes ($20 000), time contributions of staff ($6 000) and secretarial costs which can be charged against instructional costs ($2 400).

[2]Time contributions of members of the Steering Committee.

[3]This represents the employment of a Project Administrator and research assistants, and honorariums for staff members involved in the project beyond what could be expected for instructional purposes and for contributions to the profession.

[4]The printing and mailing of questionnaires and the printing of draft and final reports.

[5]Computer costs which can legitimately be charged to instruction.

[6]Travel costs for members of the Steering Committee.

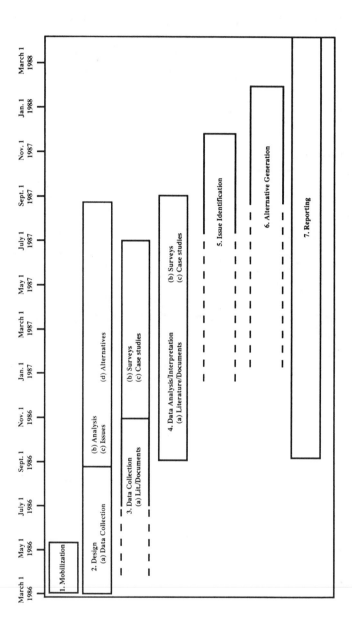

Figure 1 School Administration in Transition Phasing and Timing

A Project Proposal

An Evaluation of the Senior Administrative Structure of the Rundle School District

Prepared by

R. F. Black
W. C. Handle
S. S. Jacks
N. Sloan
L. M. Wilks

for

The Board of Trustees of the Rundle School District

August 1987

Department of Educational Administration
Provincial University

Proposal to Conduct an Evaluation of the Administrative Structure of the Rundle School District

Backdrop

This proposal is based on the understanding that the Board of Trustees of the Rundle School District wishes to have its senior management structure, excluding the performance of the senior managers, evaluated; that the evaluation is to be contracted to an external agency; that the evaluation is to be completed by April of 1988; and that the costs are to be kept to a maximum of $30 000.

The successful execution of any study requires that both parties to the contract be in agreement as to the purpose and parameters of the study, the meaning of key terms, the study objectives, the general study design, the management of the study, the time lines, and the overall budget and financial management for the study. The proposal which follows deals with all of these matters.

Purpose and Parameters of the Study

The purpose of this study is to conduct an evaluation of the management structure of the Rundle School District. The evaluation is to be limited to the senior management structure for the District and, therefore, is to exclude the evaluation of the administrative structures of schools and specific programs. The evaluation is also to be limited to the structures themselves and, therefore, is not to include the performance of personnel.

1. *Administrative Structure*

It is the understanding of the authors of this proposal that the term "administrative structure" refers to the policies, machinery, procedures and practices used by an organization to determine, coordinate and control its operations and facilitate the conduct of its work. The structure includes (1) offices and/or positions along with role descriptions and expectations for each office; (2) authoritative relationships, including decision-making and reporting responsibilities, of each office; (3) networks of communications, including procedures for acquiring and sharing information; and (4) the facilities and resources associated with administering the operations of the organization.

Administrative structures are established by people to control and facilitate the operation of the organization for which they have responsibility, in accordance with their interpretation of the mission and goals of the organization. The structure is also operated by people, usually a different set from those who established it, in order to control and facilitate the operation of the organization for which they have responsibility, in accordance with their interpretation of the mission and goals of the organization. If the formally established structure does not seem to work well, or does not seem to fit the style or needs of the people using it, it is usually bent to better fit their needs and purposes, and usually informal structures are created to replace or supplement the formal ones. Therefore, most organizations have both formal and informal administrative structures. The degree of "fit" between these two structures can be tight or loose, and the degree to which one supports the other can vary widely.

2. *Evaluation*

It is the understanding of the authors of this proposal that evaluation, in the context of the proposed study, would include (1) assessing the effectiveness of the senior administrative structure (formal and informal) in determining, coordinating and controlling the operations of the Rundle School District and facilitating the conduct of its work; (2) assessing the efficiency of the administrative structure (formal and informal) in determining, coordinating and controlling the operations of the Rundle School District and facilitating the conduct of its work; (3) determining the degree of "fit" and "supportiveness" between the formal and informal administrative structures; (4) generating alternative structures, or structural elements; and, if appropriate, (5) recommending alternative administrative structures, or structural elements, to the Board for its consideration.

Study Objectives

In order to carry out the purposes of the evaluation it would be the objective of the authors of this proposal to

1. mobilize an evaluation team;
2. develop the specific designs for the evaluation;
3. gather demographic, descriptive and historical data about the District;
4. gather data on the administrative structure of the District;
5. gather data about the philosophy, mission, goals and operations of the District;
6. gather research and literature dats on administrative structures;

7. determine legislative and regulatory constraints on administrative structures;

8. analyze and interpret the data collected in respect to Objectives 3 to 7 above;

9. determine the issues facing the District in respect to its administrative structure;

10. generate and test alternative administrative structures, or structural elements;

11. develop recommendations to be made to the Board; and

12. prepare and present a report on the evaluation study to the Board.

Study Design

Developing the specific designs for conducting a study is part of the study itself. The research team should also become familiar with the system to be evaluated before the design is completed. Therefore, the specific design for conducting the project cannot and should not be finalized until after the contract is awarded. In addition, the design should be kept flexible so as to take advantage of new information and unanticipated conditions which arise during the conduct of the project. However, an overall approach to the evaluation and some probable procedures can be developed. These are outlined below.

1. Design Model

The overall approach to conducting an evaluation project generally taken by the authors of this proposal is depicted in graphic form in Figure 1. The major steps include (1) preparing and presenting the overall proposal; (2) developing the specific designs; (3) gathering data; (4) analyzing and interpreting the data; (5) making assessments and identifying the issues; (6) generating and testing alternatives and recommendations; and (7) preparing and presenting of the report. A progress report is made to the Steering Committee for the project following phases (2), (4), (5) and (7).

2. Conceptual Frameworks

It is proposed that the specific designs for data collection, analysis, interpretation, assessment, issue identification and alternative development be based on a set of concepts previously developed by members of the proposed evaluation team to guide the evaluation of organizations, or components of organizations. For the purposes of this proposed study these concepts are drawn together into two related frameworks. One of these has to do with identifying the work and responsibilities of a school system, and the other has to do with the processes of making assessments.

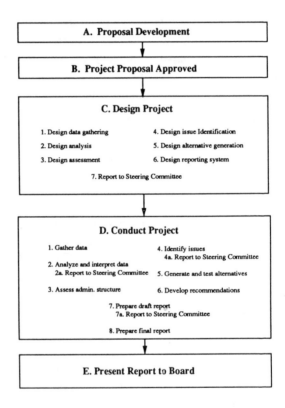

Figure 1

**Evaluation of the Administrative Structure
of the Rundle School District**

Project Design Model

COMPONENTS

	Community Relations	Student Services	Instructional Programs	Personnel	Financial Management	Support Services	Governance	Administration	Overall
Mission Philosophy Goal									
Policy									
Planning									
Program operations									
Monitoring Evaluation									
Overall									

FUNCTIONS

Senior Administrative Structure Sub-Component of Administration

Figure 2

Evaluation of the Administrative Structure of the Rundle School District

Functions and Components Model to Guide Data Gathering

The Functions and Components Model. Although the work of an educational system can be conceptualized in many ways, the Functions and Components categorization system depicted in Figure 2 has been used effectively by the authors of this proposal in other evaluations they have conducted which were similar to the one being requested by the Rundle School District. The model subdivides the responsibilities of a school system into the five functions shown on the vertical axis of Figure 2 – (1) mission, philosophy and goal development, (2) policy development, (3) planning, (4) program implementation and operation, and (5) monitoring and evaluation. These functions are performed for the eight components shown on the horizontal axis – (1) community relations, (2) student services, (3) instructional programs, (4) personnel, (5) financial management, (6) support services, (7) governance, and (8) administration - and for the system as a whole. Typically, the Board of Trustees, in carrying our the governance function, establishes the philosophy, the long-range goals and the policies for the system. It also retains responsibility for the monitoring and evaluation functions, especially in respect to the senior administration and the overall operation of the system. It also performs all other functions related to the governance component. All other functions are usually delegated to the administration, schools and teachers.

In order to assess the senior administrative structure of the Rundle School District, information on the operation of the District will have to be collected, as will similar types of information from the literature and other sources. It is proposed that the model outlined above, suitably modified to fit the situation, be used to guide this process.

Assessment Model. There are four aspects to the proposed assessment model: (1) the sub-components to be assessed; (2) the information to be used in making the assessment; (3) the assessment questions; and (4) how the assessments are to be made. The sub-components of the formal administrative structure to be assessed include the policies guiding the operation of the administrative structure; the regulations and procedures governing the operation, the offices and roles; the authoritative relationships; the communications networks; and the supporting facilities and resources. The expectations, relationships, procedures and communications networks of the informal administrative structure will also be assessed. The information and factors to be applied in making assessments include the structure, demographics, local conditions, traditions, and history of the District; the mission, philosophy, and goals of the District; survey information on the operations of the District (application of the Functions and Components Model); information from research and the literature on administrative structures;

stakeholder views and opinions on actual and preferred administrative structures; provincial legislation and regulations; and the background knowledge and orientations of the evaluators.

The assessment questions to be asked include the following. (1) How compatible is the administrative structure (and each of its sub-components) with the mission, philosophy and goals of the District? (2) How effective and efficient, within the terms of the District's mission, philosophy and goals, is the administrative structure, and each of its components, in determining, coordinating and controlling the operations of the system and facilitating the conduct of its work? (3) What is the degree of "fit" and "supportiveness" between the formal and informal administrative structures? The assessments will be made by a panel consisting of the evaluation team and invited consultants. Assessments will be made on a 5-point scale ranging from "very effective/efficient" to "very ineffective/inefficient. Figure 3 summarizes the proposed assessment process.

It is proposed that the assessment model outlined above, suitably modified to fit the particular needs of this study, be used to guide the assessment of the senior administrative structure of the Rundle School District.

3. *Study Procedures*

Although, as suggested earlier in this proposal, the specific procedures to be used cannot be finalized until the contract is awarded and an initial investigation of the system has been made, the following would be given first consideration.

Data Gathering. Data would be gathered from several sources and in several ways:

1. Information on the District, how it operates and particularly on the administrative structure would be gathered by means of document searches and interviews with Board members, senior administrators, and a sample of administrators, principals, teachers, and possibly other stakeholders.

2. Opinions respecting the actual and preferred operation of the senior administrative structure will be obtained through interviews with the same sample suggested in (1) above, and possibly through a more widely based opinionnaire (e.g., administrators, principals, and a sampling of teachers and parents).

3. Information on administrative structures in other similar systems and the research and expert opinion regarding administrative structures which members of the team already possess will be gathered through literature searches and possibly through interviews with representatives from

other systems and experts in the field, as well as through a review of documents from other systems.

4. Provincial legislation and regulations pertaining to administrative structures will be obtained through a review of documents and interviews with provincial officials.

The . . .	Evaluation Team assisted by consultants . . .
makes assessments of . . .	the following components of the *formal* senior administrative structure: 1. policies, regulations, 2. offices and roles, 3. authoritative relationships, 4. communications networks, and 5. the supporting facilities and resources; and the expectations, relationships, procedures and communications networks of the *informal* administrative structure. . .
by seeking answers to these questions:	1. How compatible are the components with the mission, philosophy and goals? 2. How efficient are the administrative structure and each of its components? 3. How effective are the administrative structure and each of its components? 4. How compatible are the formal and informal administrative structures?
through the application of this information:	1. the size, demographics, history and operations of the District; 2. the District's mission, philosophy and goals; 3. research and literature on administrative structures; 4. opinions of stakeholders; 5. Provincial legislation and regulations; and 6. the knowledge and orientations of the evaluators.

Figure 3

**Evaluation of the Administrative Structure
of the Rundle School District**

Assessment Model

Data Analysis and Interpretation. The Functions and Components Model and the Assessment Model will be used to guide the analysis, synthesis and interpretation of the data collected.

Assessment. The Assessment Model outlined above, or some modification of it, will be used in making assessments of the senior administrative structure.

Issue Identification. Following the assessment of the senior administrative structure of the District the evaluation team (with the assistance of invited consultants) will identify the issues facing the Rundle School District in its efforts to develop and maintain the most effective and efficient administrative structure possible. Issues, for the purpose of this type of evaluation, are defined as either conditions which cannot be changed but which must be taken into account in establishing and operating an administrative structure, or as constraints which can and must be removed in order to establish and/or maintain the most effective and efficient administrative structure.

Alternatives and Recommendations. The evaluation team will generate alternative administrative structures, or structural elements, for consideration of the Board, after taking into account the (1) mission, philosophy, goals, history, traditions and operations of the District; (2) the assessment made of the administrative structure; (3) the research and literature in the field; and (4) the issues identified, the evaluation team will generate alternative administrative structures, or structural elements, for the consideration of the Board. The present structure is always considered one of these alternatives. The alternatives generated will be evaluated by a panel consisting of the evaluation team and invited consultants. If appropriate, recommendations respecting a specific administrative structure, or structural elements, will be made to the Board.

Reporting. It is proposed that the evaluation team report to a Steering Committee established by the Board
1. following the finalization of the specific design by the evaluation team – to obtain feedback and overall approval of the design;
2. following the analysis and interpretation of data on the District – to obtain reactions and suggestions;
3. following assessment and issue identification – to obtain reactions and suggestions; and
4. following preparation of the draft report – to obtain reactions and suggestions.

It is also proposed that a final written report covering all aspects of the study be presented to the Board at the conclusion of the study. The final

report would include the following:
1. an executive summary;
2. a description of the background to, and design of, the study;
3. the analyzed and interpreted data about the system and its administrative structure;
4. the relevant information from the literature review;
5. the assessment of the senior administrative structure;
6. the issues faced by the system in respect to administrative structures;
7. alternative administrative structures; and
8. recommendations.

Management of the Study

The study will be conducted by a team consisting of Drs. R. F. Black, W. C. Handle, S. S. Jacks, N. Sloan, and L. M. Wilks, all from the Department of Educational Administration of Provincial University. Dr. Black will serve as Project Director. The proposed team has considerable expertise and experience in evaluation projects such as the one requested (see the attached Resumés). The team will be assisted by graduate students and by consultants selected for specific tasks (e. g., identifying emerging administrative practices and structures, assessment judgments, issue identification and alternative generation). The team will report to a Steering Committee named by the Board of Trustees of the Rundle School District at the times and for the purposes suggested in the "Report" section above.

Time Lines

The authors of this proposal are prepared to start the project by October 1, 1987, and to submit the final report by April 30, 1988. The time estimates for conducting the various phases of the project are contained in Figure 4.

Budget

The authors of this proposal are prepared to conduct the evaluation, as conceptualized in this proposal, for a contract price of $30 000. The cost estimates are contained in Table 1 and the accompanying Budget Notes.

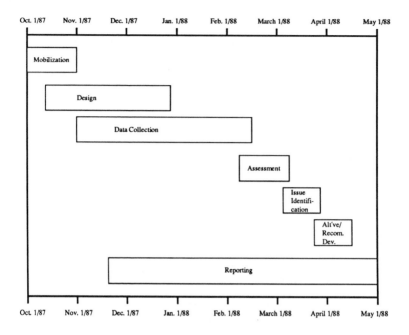

Figure 4

**Evaluation of the Administrative Structure
of the Rundle School District**

Phasing and Timing Estimates

Table 1

Evaluation of the Administrative Structure
of the Rundle School District

Budget Estimates

I. Personnel		
1. Evaluation Fee	$15 000[1]	
2. Consultant	1 500	
3. Research assistance	2 000	
4. Secretarial assistance	1 000	19 500
II. Travel/Subsistence		
5. Trips to Rundle	3 500[2]	
6. Consultants, meetings, etc.	1 500	5 000
III. Printing/Telephone/Supplies		2 500
IV. Computing		1 000
V. Overhead		2 000
Total		$30 000

[1]The Research Fee does not cover the total manpower costs estimated to conduct the study. However, because parts of the study will be used for instructional purposes (a case study for system evaluation and project design and management) a portion of the manpower costs ($6 600) will be absorbed by the Department of Educational Administration. Total manpower expenditure by the evaluation team, exclusive of consultants and research assistants, is estimated at 72 days, or a dollar expenditure of $2 600.

[2]It is estimated that one person will make two one-day visits to Rundle, that two people will make six one-day visits to Rundle and that four people will make one three-day visit to Rundle.

Appendix C

Data Gathering Frameworks

Table 1
INMATE EDUCATION PROGRAM
Data Gathering Framework -- Phases 2 and 3

Evaluation Objectives	Data Needs		Data Collection	
	Types	Location	Means	Notes
1. Monitoring				
(i) To monitor the Inmate Education Program at the provincial level with respect to its objectives, context, inputs, development, structures, functions, activities, relationships, and outcomes.	(a) Documents, minutes, reports, literature, etc.	(a) Advanced Education, Solicitor-General's office, Alberta Education.	(a) Document searches.	(a) Arranged through appropriate officials of the Program and the other agencies involved. The initial search for contextual and developmental data carried out early in the project. Arrangements made with the appropriate officials for the collection of monitoring data throughout the life of the pilot program.
	(b) Recollections and opinions of involved and knowledgeable persons.	(b) Officials in Advanced Education, the Solicitors-General's office, Alberta Education, and from other involved organizations and agencies which might be identified. Members of the Programs' Advisory Committee. Officials of organizations such as the John Howard Society.	(b) Interviews.	(b) Interviews held early in the project with the key officials in the program and with members of the Advisory Committee. Other individuals are identified through this process. They are also interviewed early in the project. Arrangements are made for follow-up interviews with all appropriate individuals.

Table 1 (continued)

Evaluation Objectives	Data Needs		Data Collection	
	Types	Location	Means	Notes
	(c) Dynamics of the ongoing activities and deliberations.	(c) Advisory Committee meetings. Meetings or programs of other relevant groups.	(c) Observations.	(c) Arrangements are made early in the project for members of the Evaluating Team to attend and observe appropriate meetings and activities throughout the life of the program.
(ii) To monitor, at the institutional level, Inmate Education programs with respect to objectives, context, inputs, development, structures, functions, activities, relationships, and outcomes.	(a) Same as in (i)a.	(a) As in (i)a, plus consortium members in each location.	(a) As in (i)a.	(a) As in (i)a.
	(b) Same as in (i)b.	(b) As in (i)b, plus involved members of the consortiums in each location, instructors and inmates.	(b) As in (i)b.	(b) As in (i)b.
	(c) Same as in (i)c.	(c) Meetings of local advisory committees. Activities of other relevant consortium groups.	(c) As in (i)c.	(c) As in (i)c.

Table 1 (continued)

Evaluation Objectives	Data Needs		Data Collection	
	Types	Location	Means	Notes
(iii) To monitor projects (with the exception of those delivered by school boards) with respect to their objectives, inputs, contexts, development, structures, functions, activities, relationships, and outcomes.	(a) As in (i)a. (b) As in (i)b. (c) As in (i)c.	(a) As in (ii)a, plus instructors and students. (b) As in (ii)b. (c) As in (ii)c, plus class activities.	(a) Document searches including class outlines, schedules, assignments, student records, etc. (b) Interviews. (c) Observations.	(a) As in (i)a, with emphasis on those directly involved in each project and the delivering agency. (b) As in (i)b, with emphasis on the delivering agency and the instructors. (c) As in (i)c, with emphasis on project activities.
2. Analysis To analyze the data collected in the monitoring activities at each of the three levels: provincial level, institutional level and project level, and to evaluate the program primarily from a formative orientation, but with some attention to summative evaluation.	(a) Data from the monitoring activities for objective 1 (i), (ii), and (iii) above.	(a) Reports from evaluation team members responsible for monitoring activities.	(a) Documents. Case study analysis techniques. Quantitative analysis when appropriate. Other means seen as appropriate after initial examination of the data.	(a) Initial analysis should be done early in the project (after contextual and developmental data have been collected). An analysis for the purposes of formative evaluation should be prepared for the conclusion of Phase 2. An analysis for the purpose of both summative and formative evaluation should be completed for the conclusion of Phase 3.

Table 1 (continued)

Evaluation Objectives	Data Needs		Data Collection	
	Types	Location	Means	Notes
	(b) Decisions relative to analysis model(s).	(b) Records of decision of the evaluation team.	(b) Document searches.	(b) The decision regarding the evaluation model(s) to be used initially will be made early in the project. Modifications may be made after initial examination of the data.
	(c) Literature on program evaluation.	(c) Libraries and persons knowledgeable about evaluation and analysis.	(c) Literature searches. Interviews.	(c) Literature searches and interviews regarding evaluation models, approaches, techniques, and devices will be made early in the project.
3. Issues				
To generate issues surrounding Inmate Education at the three levels.	(a) Data from the monitoring activities. The data analysis.	(a) Reports from evaluation team members responsible for monitoring and analysis.	(a) Data reports 1 (i), (ii), (iii) and 2. Seminars. Interviews.	(a) The first set of issues will be generated for the report on Phase 2, as one of the outcomes of the formative evaluation. The second set will be generated for the report on Phase 3 and the total project.
	(b) Literature on inmate education.	(b) Libraries and agencies involved in inmate education.	(b) Literature searches. Interviews.	(b)
	(c) Information and models on issue identification.	(c) Libraries and individuals knowledgeable about issue identification.	(c) Literature searches. Interviews.	(c)

Table 1 (continued)

Evaluation Objectives	Data Needs		Data Collection	
	Types	Location	Means	Notes
4. Alternative Delivery Systems To develop and test alternative delivery systems for inmate education.	(a) Documents containing research, experiences, and views on inmate education. (b) Documents regarding policies, resources, constraints, etc. of the involved organizations and agencies. (c) Opinions and views of involved and knowledgeable individuals. (d) Data on the monitoring, analysis, and issues generating phases of the inmate education evaluation study. (e) Models and information on the generation and testing of alternatives.	(a) Libraries; involved and knowledgeable agencies and individuals. (b) The Attorney General's office, Alberta Advanced Education, Alberta Education, the delivering agencies, the correctional institutions involved, etc. (c) Decision makers from the involved institutions and agencies. Experts in the field. (d) Records and reports from the inmate education evaluation study. (e) Libraries and knowledgeable people	(a) Document and library searches. (b) Document searches. (c) Interviews. (d) Document searches. (e) Library searches. Interviews.	(a) (b) The development and testing of alternatives will not be completed until near the end of the evaluation project. (c) However, the collection of data and the development of the system for development and testing (d) will be completed much earlier. (e)

Table 1 (continued)

Evaluation Objectives	Data Needs		Data Collection	
	Types	Location	Means	Notes
5. Reporting				
(i) To provide periodic program reports to the Advisory Committee on Inmate Education and to the Department of Advanced Education.	(a) Research and management reports on the evaluation project.	(a) Records and files of the evaluation project.	(a) Document searches.	(a) A regular system for presenting progress reports will be arranged with the Advisory Committees and Alberta Advanced Education.
(ii) At the conclusion of each phase and at the end of the evaluation project, to prepare a written report for the Department of Advanced Education.	(b) Views of the evaluation team members.	(b) Members of the evaluation team.	(b) Interviews and seminars.	(b) Written reports will be presented to Alberta Education, the Advisory Committees, and the institutions involved at the end of each phase and at the completion of the evaluation project.

Table 2
EDUCATION NORTH EVALUATION
Data Gathering System

Objective	Data Needs	Data Sources	Means of Collection
1. Monitoring			
(i) To monitor the operations of Education North with respect to its structures, functions, activities, and relationships.	(a) Documents, minutes, letters, etc. related to the development and operation of Education North.	(a) Education North files. Relevant files in other offices.	(a) Document searches.
	(b) The recollections and views of involved individuals.	(b) Education North staff, Minister's Advisory Committee, relevant staff from government departments, leaders from local societies and school systems, etc.	(b) Interviews.
	(c) Activites of the Project.	(c) Minister's Advisory Committee, Education North staff.	(c) Observations, diaries, and interviews.
(ii) To monitor the operations of the local societies established by Education North with respect to their structures, functions, activities, and relationships.	(a) Documents, minutes, letters, etc. related to the development and operation of each local project.	(a) Education North files and the files of local societies.	(a) Document searches.
	(b) Recollections and views of involved individuals.	(b) Education North staff, members of local societies, Minister's Advisory Committee, etc.	(b) Interviews.
	(c) Activities of the projects.	(c) Society meetings, other activities, functions, etc.	(c) Observations and interviews.

Table 2 (continued)

Objective	Data Needs	Data Sources	Means of Collection
2. Evaluating			
(i) To assess the structures, functions, activities, relationships and outcomes of Education North with respect to the explicit and implicit objectives of the project.	(a) Objectives of Education North.	(a) Data collected for 1(i) above as these relate to objectives.	(a) Data reports for 1(i).
	(b) Assessment of the projects of local societies with respect to the objectives established by Education North.	(b) Data collected for 2(ii) below.	(b) Reports for 2(ii) below.
	(c) Information on the experiences of similar projects.	(c) Libraries and information banks.	(c) Library searches.
	(d) Information on project operations.	(d) Data collected for 1(i) above.	(d) Data reports for 1(i) above.
(ii) To assess the structures, functions, activities, relationships and outcomes of the projects undertaken by the local societies with respect to the explicit and implicit objectives established for the projects by Education North.	(a) Objectives of Education North as they relate to local projects.	(a) Data collected for 1(i) as they relate to objectives.	(a) Data reports for 1(i).
	(b) Structures, functions, activities and relationships of local projects.	(b) Data collect for 1(ii) above.	(b) Data reports for 1(ii).
	(c) Indicators of achievement or movement toward the objectives.	(c) Documents and records in school and community files. Students, teachers, adults, project staff, Education North staff.	(c) Document searches. Questionnaires and Interviews.

Table 2 (continued)

Objective	Data Needs	Data Sources	Means of Collection
2. Evaluating (continued)			
(iii) To assess the impact of the evaluation activities on the operations and outcomes of the projects of local societies and the overall project.	(a) Opinions of involved individuals.	(a) Project staff, Minister's Advisory Committee, Steering Committee, local project people, and the evaluators.	(a) Interviews, questionnaires.
	(b) Experiences in similar projects.	(b) Literature on evaluation and interventions.	(b) Literature searches.
3. Consulting			
To provide consultative assistance to local societies with respect to the "internal evaluation" of their projects.	(a) The objectives, structures, functions, and relationships of local projects.	(a) Data collected for 1(ii) above.	(a) Data reports for 1(ii) above.
	(b) Opinions, views, plans, and resources for local evaluation.	(b) Members of local societies, Education North staff.	(b) Interviews, observations, documents.
4. Reporting			
(i) To provide informal progress reports to each meeting of the Minister's Advisory Committee for Education North.	(a) Activities, plans, and outcomes of the evaluation activities relevant for the particular report.	(a) Persons involved in the evaluation.	(a) Reports, interviews.

Table 2 (continued)

Objective	Data Needs	Data Sources	Means of Collection
4. Reporting (continued)			
(ii) To provide progress reports and seek advice from the Steering Committee established for Education North.			
(iii) To provide annual reports and a final report to Alberta Education.			
(iv) To produce a handbook based on the experiences and findings of the project evaluation, and on relevant literature, to assist educators and community development workers to select effective ways of working in similar settings.	(a) All data and findings for evaluation objectives 1-3. (b) Experiences in similar projects and opinions concerning programs similar to Education North.	(a) The individuals involved in the evaluation. (b) Libraries and information banks.	(a) All reports, interviews. (b) Literature searches.

Appendix D
Issue Statement

Blue Mountain School Division
Attendance Area Study

Underlying Issues

Issue Identification

A major function in any policy review process is to identify the issues that have an impact on the situation, because to be effective, a policy must help resolve the issue or at the very least take the issue into account. Issues can be defined in terms of the two factors contributing to their creation – contingencies and constraints.

Contingencies are subject to change in the short- or mid-term. Those internal to the system, or under the control of the system, are relatively easy to modify, for example, a policy related to making decisions about bus routes. A contingency external to the system, or under the control of some other agency is more difficult for the system to modify, because it requires negotiations with another body, for example, the upgrading of roads to accommodate school buses.

Constraints are either not subject to change or, if they can be changed, it is with great difficulty and in most cases over the long term. An example of an internal constraint which can be changed, but only over a long time, would be the present school facilities and school buses. External constraints which are not subject to change, especially by efforts of the school system, would be the population mix of the area and the physical geography of the Division.

An analysis and interpretation of the data collected for this study revealed several issues which have an impact on attendance areas, busing and the delivery of education to the residents of the Blue Mountain School Division. Some of these issues can be categorized as constraints, whereas others are categorized as contingencies.

Constraint Issues not Subject to Change

The following issues are constraints to any attempt to modify attendance area, busing, or educational delivery policy. Although the issues themselves cannot be changed by the school system, they must be taken into account in developing or implementing policy.

Geographic characteristics

There are many geographic characteristics which affect the delivery of education in the Blue Mountain School Division. Most of these are not subject to change, although their effects can be modified by communication and transportation technology. The natural boundaries of the Division, including the Blue Mountains on the north, the relatively unsettled area on the south, and the provincial border on the west, all affect the accessibility to schools and the way in which education must be delivered. The several deep valleys which affected settlement patterns and transportation routes, especially in earlier times, have created areas of relative isolation and therefore, have had a major effect on how education has been and is delivered. The two major highways which divide the Blue Mountain Division into four quadrants affect the shopping and social movement of people, as does the presence of Donway near the western boundary and Fox River and Craig near the eastern boundary.

Discussion. These geographic features have affected education by creating several semi-isolated communities which, by their very nature, develop strong feelings of community loyalty. At the same time, the sparse population in some areas and the geographic barriers created by the rivers and the valleys have made the delivery of education more expensive and difficult. The improvement of communication and transportation, on the other hand, has changed shopping and travel patterns, and the life style of most people in the regions. Therefore, a breakdown in the traditional way of life in most of the communities is taking place, including how education is structured and delivered. Conflict within individuals, between individuals, and between groups has predictably developed in respect to the centralization of the delivery of school programs and the overall philosophy of education.

These conditions cannot be readily changed, nor can the issues they give rise to be readily resolved. Therefore, in the short term at least, they can only be taken into account in developing educational policies and programs.

Social and Cultural Characteristics The social, cultural and economic characteristics of the people also have a major impact upon their philosophy of education and the way they see their wants and their educational needs. These characteristics of the people in the Blue Mountain School Division have been shaped in part by the geography of the region, and also by the backgrounds of the various communities and the culture of the people.

Discussion. The relative isolation of some communities, combined with the agricultural economy of the area, has contributed to strong feelings of community and self-reliance. The declining rural population and, therefore, the decline in school enrollments in the rural communities, combined with the sociological phenomenon of "the expanding community" (created by the increasing ease of communications with, and transportation to, larger centres) has caused great concern throughout the region. This, in turn, has caused differences in educational and social philosophies to surface. On the one extreme are those who want their children to benefit from the advantages that they believe can only be obtained from larger schools, which can only be found in the larger centres. Maintaining the life style of the small community is not a major priority. On the other extreme are those who believe that the small community and the rural way of life have much to recommend them. This way of life will be lost if the schools are centralized further. The small communities and the small schools, they believe, must be retained. In most respects, they believe the smaller community school provide a superior education.

As is the case with the geographic characteristics of the region, the social and cultural characteristics cannot be readily changed in the short term; however, they must be taken into account in developing educational policies and programs for the Division.

Language and Religious Differences

Canadian history is rife with cases of educational conflict and problems that arise from language and religious differences. The minority language and/or religious groups attempt to further their interests through the education of the youth. If they cannot do this through the public school system – to the extent they wish – they attempt to modify the system, establish private schools, or send their children to other jurisdictions. This, in turn, creates conflicts with the majority group, who see the public system eroded by these moves. These conditions exist in several communities in the Blue Mountain School Division.

Discussion. The desires of the francophone population in the Cadotte area to have their children educated in the French language and culture and the creation of private religious schools in the Wingate and Coxville areas are examples of how language and religious differences can affect the delivery of education. In each of these cases, these differences have caused a decline in the public school population. This decline in enrollment has affected the program and is endangering the existence of some of the schools.

Although the way in which education is delivered and whether compulsory attendance to public schools can be modified, the underlying wants and the needs created by religious and cultural differences are not readily modified. In the short term these differences can only be taken into account in establishing educational policies and practices.

Constraint Issues Subject to Change

The following issues are subject to change over the long term. However, in the short term there are constraints which must be taken into account in developing and implementing school attendance area, busing and educational delivery policy.

Location and Nature of Facilities

The presence and nature of buildings and other facilities are a constraint to changes in the educational program and its delivery. The structure and layout of buildings dictate, to a large measure, the nature of the program. The presence of buildings in a particular location also dictates, to a large measure, the educational delivery to that location. In other words, it would be difficult to make major modifications in the location of educational delivery when major facilities already exist.

Discussion. The presence of school buildings and facilities in the present centres in the Blue Mountain School Division makes it difficult to effect major changes in attendance areas or the location of new schools or school additions. For example, it would be very difficult to close the schools at Coxville and Berry River and build a new one at Greenville, even if this seemed to be the best long-term solution to providing education in the east end of the Division. *We are not suggesting that this is the best solution but are only using this as an example of how the existence of facilities acts as a constraint on policies regarding delivery locations.*

Although it would be possible to change the delivery of educational programs to different locations in the Blue Mountain School Division from those that exist now, it would be very difficult to do so, at least in the short term. Therefore, the present facilities and their location must be taken into account in developing or modifying educational policies, educational programs and their delivery. However, the nature of these facilities is open to modification.

Composition of Bus Fleet

Modifications in transportation policy and programs are affected in large measure by the extent and nature of the bus fleet. For example, it would be difficult in the short term to change from a few long bus routes which require large buses, to several shorter routes which require small buses. The cost would be prohibitive.

Discussion. Any major changes in transportation policy in the Blue Mountain School Division and the programs developed to effect this policy would have to be implemented slowly so that modifications in the bus fleet could be made in an efficient and effective manner. In fact, the Blue Mountain School Division is gradually changing from large to small buses. However, modifications in the transportation grants for 1986/87 may make it possible to modify practices to some extent (for example, load factor changes which provide full grants for two junior or senior high school students per seat, plus increased per diem grants for short routes).

School Grants

The various educational grants provided by the provincial government, plus the regulations and traditions governing supplementary requisitions, also act as constraints on the development of educational policies and programs by local school jurisdictions.

Discussion. The restraint program in the province and the reluctance of local ratepayers to see their taxes increased are certainly a constraint on the availability of funds and, therefore, on how much money the Blue Mountain School Division can allocate to new programs, or to the provision of other services. It would indeed to difficult to add new programs without cutting out existing programs, or without making economies in present operations.

In developing new policies and programs, one must take into account the extent and nature of the grant program as well as the ability of the System to raise local revenues.

Differing Philosophies of Education

Beliefs concerning the purposes of education and how education should be delivered create powerful constraints on a school board. These constraints are magnified if there are two or more strong and divergent belief systems in the community.

Discussion. There are at least two divergent philosophies held by a substantial number of people in the Blue Mountain School Division. One group holds the position that the larger schools, because they have more human and material resources, can provide a richer and more varied educational experience. They also believe that their children should have the opportunities to benefit from these experiences. The inconvenience of longer bus rides is one of the disadvantages they must put up with for the sake of a better education for their children.

The other major philosophic position is that rural communities and the rural way of life must be preserved. Children will benefit most in the long run if they can receive their education, or most of it at least, in the home community. "Small" can also be good, because it allows for the recognition of the individual and his or her place in the community. Those holding this philosophic position also believe that education can be delivered just as effectively, if not more effectively, and probably just as efficiently in the small communities where the people live.

These differing philosophies may change over time, but in the short- to mid-term they both must be taken into account in the development of educational policies and programs.

Contingency Issues

Most of the following issues can be dealt with by the school system itself in a relatively short time period. Others require the collaboration of other agencies.

School Attendance Area Policies and Practice

The present practices in regard to a particular issue always act as a constraint on the process of considering other policies. In many respects, an organization becomes relatively comfortable with its present policies, and so do its participants and clients. In other words, they have accommodated to the way the organization operates. Even though the policies and the practices growing out of them may be causing problems, there will still be resistance to modifying them. People generally feel more secure with the known, even though they may not like it, than with the unknown.

Discussion. Although most parents in the Blue Mountain School Division seem to be satisfied with the schools their children are attending and would not choose to send them to other schools, there is still strong support for an "open attendance area" policy. On the other hand, a large minority of parents believe that children should be sent to the school in their attendance area. They believe that an erosion of this policy will result in the loss of the school and, therefore, many small rural communities.

There was also a concern expressed by several parents that the Board allows some children to attend outside schools, whereas it does not allow others who seem to have equally compelling reasons to do so. From reports received, it would seem that most parents who send their children to Conway and Fox River would like to have this privilege continued, whereas a number of others believe that the children of the Division should be educated in the Division.

In order to develop a policy that will satisfy, to some extent at least, the interests of all these parents, their concerns will have to be carefully considered and innovative modifications in attendance area policy developed.

Transportation Policies and Practices

Policies on attendance areas and transportation of students are, of necessity, closely related. However, there are transportation policies which are relatively unrelated to the attendance area question, for example, pick-up points, order of pick-up and drop-off, and bus comfort and safety.

Discussion. Although most parents were relatively satisfied with the transportation policies and practices of the Blue Mountain School Division, there were some concerns expressed by a fairly large minority of parents – mainly in the interviews. These included concerns about time on the bus, comfort on the bus, the nature of the route, and the time of pick-up and drop-off. The major complaint of those who were concerned was the lack of information and involvement in respect to determining busing practice in their area. These concerns should be given careful consideration in any review of transportation policies and practices. The use of computerized bus routing programs, such as those described to the Superintendent and Superintendent of Busing, also makes bus routing more efficient and effective.

The Nature of Education and Its Delivery

The way people view the purposes of education and how it should be delivered will determine in large measure how they view attendance areas, transportation of students and the operation of the schools. As discussed above, the philosophies of education held by people cannot be readily changed. However, the nature of the programs and how they are delivered are more open to modification.

Discussion. Although most parents are satisfied with their schools, they do not want to see further centralization. In fact, a large minority would prefer to see more schools built. They would also like to see new programs such as vocational education introduced into the Division's schools. There is, however, a sizable minority who are dissatisfied with the schools, some because they do not provide the type of well-rounded community education children need, others because they do not take advantage of new ideas and technologies which would make it easier to deliver quality education to small numbers of students in small rural communities.

This concern about the nature of education and its delivery is probably the most important issue underlying the concerns about attendance areas and transportation. It should become a high priority issue for the Board.

Road and Transportation Upgrading

The establishment and modification of attendance areas and bus routes depend in no small measure on the quality of the roads and the willingness of the municipal authorities to cooperate with the school authorities. However, the development of improved transportation and communications technologies can also have an effect on how attendance areas and bus routes can be modified.

Discussion. The location and quality of the roads in the Blue Mountain School Division played a major role in determining the present attendance areas and bus routes. Although the roads in most areas of the Division have been improved over the years, they still determine, in some cases, where buses cannot travel in safety. However, the application of improved communication technologies may make it possible to modify routes and still adhere to appropriate safety standards.

Administrative Policies and Practices

People are often as concerned about the way decisions are made and their role in the decision-making process as they are with the decisions themselves. However, it is also true that people who are dissatisfied with a policy or a program will also express dissatisfaction with the process. In any case, this phenomenon can create serious problems in the operation of any organization.

Discussion. Many of those interviewed who expressed dissatisfaction with aspects of education also expressed dissatisfaction with the planning, decision-making, and communication processes. However, several who were generally satisfied with the educational system also indicated some degree of dissatisfaction with certain aspects of planning, policy making, and public communication. These concerns could develop into a major issue affecting all other issues discussed above if corrective action is not taken.

Appendix E

A Conceptual Framework

Excerpt from
Building School-Community Relationships in Northern Communities

A Conceptual Framework

The development of a set of policies and the design of a program to implement these policies can be greatly facilitated and the end product significantly improved if some time is devoted to developing an appropriate framework or model to give shape, substance, and direction to the policies.

A model or a framework is a simplified representation of that part of reality which is of concern to the policy developer, just as a road map of Jasper National Park is a simplified version of reality for a person merely wishing to travel through the park, or a floor plan of a commercial building is a representation of the reality of the building for a person wishing to locate a particular office. For example, the social systems model may represent the reality of the structure and relationships of a school for someone wishing to study school climate.

In order for a model to be of value to a policy developer or decision maker, the relevant parts (concepts) making up the significant reality as well as the structure (relationships) tying these parts together must be identified. Models can also include predictive relationships which forecast behavior or its consequences.

The application of a relevant model for policy and program development is useful for three major reasons: (1) it assists in identifying the factors and issues which should be considered in developing the particular policies and programs of concern at the time; (2) it suggests patterns of relationships, including predictive behavior, which exist among the factors and between the system and its environment; and (3) it provides a pattern or map of key factors and the relationships among these factors, to protect against inadvertent oversight in the policy development process.

The framework suggested here is intended for use in assessing possible provincial policies and programs aimed at encouraging parents, teachers and other community members in small, isolated northern communities to work together in planning and developing activities which would better meet the educational needs of members of the communities, especially school-aged children. This framework has been derived from (1) the literature on social development, especially in Third World countries and the underdeveloped areas of developed countries; (2) the literature on organizational development and leadership; and (3) the findings of the Education

North Evaluation Project.

An Intervention Model

The experiences and findings of the evaluation of Education North, combined with the intervention literature in other similar situations, sugges three major dimensions according to which one can examine provincial intervention – that is, "setting the stage" at the local level – for the purpose of increasing adult involvement and improving the relevance and quality o educational programs. These three dimensions are *(1) the extent to which the "intervention mechanism" is associated with the formal educationa system; (2) the extent to which the intervention is either program oriente or project specific; and (3) the extent to which the intervention is controlle by provincial or other external authorities.* Each of these dimensions can be assessed according to the autonomy or degree of freedom afforded the loca community (agency or group). For example (1) if the intervention mechan ism has no formal relationships with the school, then it is highly auto nomous on that dimension; (2) if it has a very broad program focus, it i highly autonomous on that dimension; and (3) if the province provides ver little by way of advice, consultative assistance, or program and financia control, then the community is highly autonomous on that dimension.

Any particular intervention strategy can be described according to thes three dimensions. Figure 1 shows the parameters within which any strateg can be described in terms of autonomy on each of the three dimensions. Th eight strategies illustrated in Figure 1 depict polarities on one or all of th dimensions.

Strategy 1 represents a very low autonomy intervention. For example a community school with a parent advisory committee might be funded t develop a set of grade three readers focusing on local content. Alberta Edu cation plans to give considerable consultative assistance and intends t monitor the project closely. Both pre- and post-audits are built into the inter vention strategy.

On the other hand, *Strategy 8* represents a high-autonomy interventior For example, funds might be given to a broadly based community grou which has few, if any, ties with the school or school system, to conduct an type of program they wish providing it has as its objective the enhancemen of parental interest and involvement in their own and their children's educa tion. Little or no provincial control is exercised, except for that necessary t ensure financial accountability on a post-audit basis.

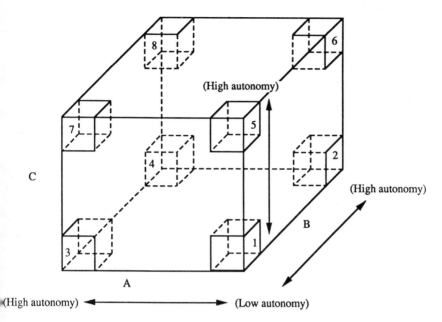

Dimensions

A. Association with the educational system in the community.

B. Degree to which the intervention is program oriented or project specific.

C. Degree of external (provincial) control.

FIGURE 1

INTERVENTION MODEL:
COMMUNITY INVOLVEMENT IN EDUCATION

Strategies 2 and 3 would be similar to *Strategy 1,* except that in No. 2 a broad program focus is approved, and in No. 3 the intervention mechanism has few, if any, formal ties to the school. *Strategy 4* represents an intervention structure with few ties to the school system and a broad program focus, but highly controlled in other ways by Alberta Education. *Strategies 6 and 7* are similar to *Strategy 8,* except that in No. 6 the structure is controlled by the school, and in No. 7 the program has a specific project focus. *Strategy 5* represents an intervention which has a specific project focus, is controlled by the school, but is relatively autonomous as far as provincial control is concerned.

Applying the Intervention Model to Specific Situations

The identification and description of intervention strategies for "stage setting" at the local level, in terms of the three-dimensional model explained

above, may be interesting from an academic point of view but are of ver
little practical value unless we can provide some direction as to which stra
tegies are most practical in specific types of communities and under specifi
conditions. In other words, *what factors should determine whic
intervention strategy should be adopted in particular communities?* Th
literature on organizational and social leadership suggests some possib
answers to this questions. The concepts of situational leadership (Hersey &
Blanchard, 1977) are particularly useful in this regard.

Early leadership studies identified two major dimensions of leadershi
behavior: (1) "task behavior," in which the leader focused on the task th
followers were to perform; and (2) "relationship behavior," in which th
leader focused on motivating his or her followers and providing psycholog
cal support for them. The relationship between these two dimensions i
shown in Figure 2. According to these concepts, the Quadrant 1, high-tas
and high-relationship, represented the most effective leadership style; Qua
drant 2, high-relationship and low-task behavior, was the next most effec
tive; and Quadrant 4, low-relationship and low-task behavior, represente
the least effective style.

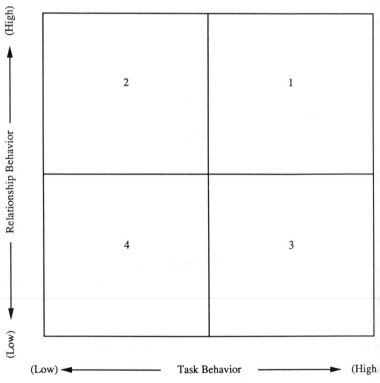

FIGURE 2

FOUR BASIC LEADERSHIP STYLES

Later leadership studies began to cast doubt on the concepts of effective leadership described above, since effective administrators were found to employ leadership styles in each of the four quadrants. These studies gave rise to situational leadership theory, which suggests that *the most effective leadership style varies from situation to situation depending upon the level of maturity of the organizational members in the area in which leadership is to be exercised.* Maturity is made up of three factors: (1) the capacity to set high and attainable goals; (2) the willingness and ability to take responsibility; and (3) the education, skill and experience in the task area. According to this theory, which is based on considerable research and experience, (1) high-task (directive) behavior and low-relationship (supportive) behavior are most effective with immature organizational members; (2) moderately to highly directive and supportive behavior is most effective with moderately mature organizational members, and (3) low-directive and supportive behavior is most effective with mature organizational members. In other words, mature people need very little by way of external leadership. Situational leaderships are depicted in Figure 3. "Delegating," (Style S_4) seems most appropriate for mature (M_4) organization members; "Participating" and "selling" (Styles S_3 and S_2) seem most appropriate for moderately mature (M_3 and M_4) organizational members; and "telling" (Style S_1) seems most appropriate for immature (M_1) organizational members.

The findings of the Education North Evaluation Project (Ingram & McIntosh, 1983), combined with the literature on social change and the application of systems theory, would suggest that the concepts of situational leadership, although developed from research in formal organizations, can also be applied to interventions (leadership) into small northern communities (organizations). In other words, situational leadership concepts derived from leadership research on formal organization can be appropriately used as a model for educational leadership interventions into small communities in northern Alberta. In doing so, however, some of the concepts need to be redefined and slightly modified.

Task and Relationship Behavior needs to be reinterpreted as follows: (1) *Task Behavior* is the provincial rules and regulations governing program approval and operations; and (2) *Relationship Behavior* is the nature of facilitative and control interventions on the part of provincial consultants and officials.

Follower(s) needs to be interpreted as the participating community (agency or group) and the members of the community.

Maturity of Followers, in a community context, would be defined as th willingness and ability of community agencies and individual members t participate in education programs, the extent and level of skills existing i the community which would permit effective participation, and the overal readiness of the community to participate (educational levels, past experi ence, motivation, etc.). *Community Readiness* would be a better term to use.

Leaders would include the provincial, or external, consultants an officials responsible for the program.

The descriptive term for the S_1 leadership style as illustrated in Figure would be changed from "telling" to "directing"; the S_2 description, "sel ling," would be change to "influencing"; the S_3 description, "participating, could be changed to "consulting;" and the S_4 description, "delegating, could be retained. The application of situational leadership theory to provin

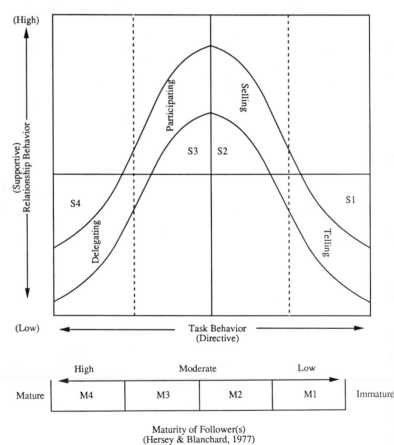

Maturity of Follower(s)
(Hersey & Blanchard, 1977)

FIGURE 3

SITUATIONAL LEADERSHIP STYLES

cial intervention in communities for the purpose of increasing community involvement in education and the relevant participation skills held by community members are represented in Figure 4.

Appropriate Intervention Styles

In a community judged to be low in readiness (R_1) for citizen participation in educational programming, an S_1 (directing) style would, according to situational leadership theory, be most appropriate.

In a community judged to be moderately ready (R_4 or R_3) for a citizen participation program, an S_2 (influencing) or an S_3 (consulting) style would seem most appropriate. An S_4 (delegating) style would seem most appropriate in a community judged ready (R_4) for a citizen participation program. Illustrative types of regulating and consultative behavior included in these styles are shown in Table 1.

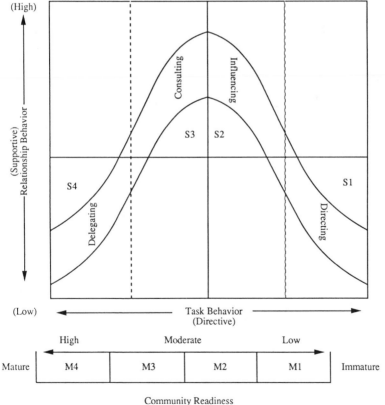

FIGURE 4

**EXTERNAL INTERVENTION STYLES
FOR ADULT PARTICIPATION IN EDUCATION**

TABLE 1

Illustrative Directive and Consultative Behavior Which Might be Appropriate for Communities with Varying Degrees of Readiness

Type of Behavior	Low	Moderate	High
Provincial Directives			
1. The program must be controlled and administered by the school system.	x		
2. The school system must approve the program.	x	x	
3. The school system must be represented on the policy body.	x	x	
4. The school system must be kept informed of program plans and activities.	x	x	
5. No regulations are made respecting association with the school system.			x
6. Only specific projects with visible end products will be approved.	x		
7. All details of the program, its operation and administration, must be spelled out in the proposal.	x	x	
8. The specifics of administration are established provincially, after consultation with local leaders.	x	x	
9. Only the objectives of the program and its general nature need to be spelled out in the proposal.			x
10. Financial control is exercised at the provincial level.	x		
11. Budget approved pre-audit and post-audit are conducted by provincial officers.	x	x	
12. Budget approval and post-audit are conducted by provincial officials.	x	x	
13. Budget approval is done by provincial officials.			x
14. No budget control except for audited annual reports is required.			x
15. Program decisions are made provincially.	x		
16. Regular reports on activities are required.	x	x	
17. Provincial officials must be consulted on all major program decisions.	x	x	
18. No program control is exercised provincially except for initial approval for funding.			x
Consultative Behavior			
1. Regular monitoring and inspection visits are made.	x	x	
2. Local program personnel are informed of errors and mistakes and are told to improve the operations.	x		
3. Leadership training programs are conducted and local personnel are expected to participate.	x	x	
4. Leadership training materials are developed and sent to local personnel, along with suggestions for their use.	x	x	
5. Consultative and monitoring visits are made regularly, but behavior is not in a control mode.	x	x	x
6. Consultative visits or contacts are made only on request.	x	x	x

In making decisions about the appropriate intervention program for a "low," "moderate," or "high" readiness community, the three-dimensional model illustrated in Figure 1 can be applied. It suggests that three major factors must be considered in any intervention program: (1) the extent of association with the school; (2) the specificity of the program of activities; and (3) the extent of external (provincial) control.

On the basis of situational leadership theory, the most appropriate intervention strategy for a "low readiness" community would seem to be one with "low autonomy" on all three dimensions of the intervention model illustrated in Figure 1. In other words, it would include a close association with the school, it would require a specific project focus, and considerable external monitoring and control would be built into the program. Strategy 1 in Figure 1 represents such a program.

On the other hand, the most appropriate strategy for a "high readiness" community would seem to be one with high autonomy on all three dimensions of the intervention model. Such a strategy would allow independence from the school, a broad program focus, and minimum provincial intervention. Strategy 8 in Figure 1 represents such a program.

The most appropriate strategies for communities with varying degrees of readiness between the "high (R_4)" and "low (R_1)" extremes would be those somewhere between the "high" and "low" autonomy positions on each of the three dimensions on the intervention model illustrated in Figure 1. It is also likely that unique situations in some communities might require a strategy which is low on some dimensions and high on others.

Typical intervention strategies – the local education society, the community school, local control, the curriculum development resource centre, the adult education strategy, the community development strategy, and consulting and facilitating – have been present in Part Two of this sourcebook. The placement of each strategy on the intervention model is illustrated in Figure 5.

It is interesting to note that each of these strategies is fairly flexible on one or two dimensions and therefore can be modified to accommodate communities with varying degrees of readiness. For example, the local education society strategy could function on a "moderate" to "high" level of autonomy on the association-with-the-school dimension, could have either a broad program or a specific project focus, and could have a "high" to "moderate" level of autonomy on the provincial control dimension. Similar variations in the other strategies can be observed in Figure 5.

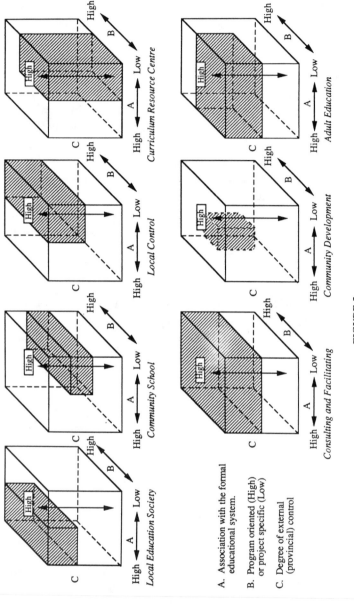

A. Association with the formal educational system.

B. Program oriented (High) or project specific (Low)

C. Degree of external (provincial) control

FIGURE 5

THE LOCATION OF COMMON INTERVENTION STRATEGIES ON THE INTERVENTION MODEL

Dimensions of Community Readiness

Thus far in our development of the operational concepts of situational leadership for community involvement in education, we have said very little about determining the level of "readiness for involvement" in communities applying to participate in a program, except that readiness is made up of three factors: (1) the ability to set high and attainable goals; (2) the willingness and ability to assume responsibility; and (3) education, skill and experience pertaining to participation in educational programming and decision making.

The level of maturity of "followers" in organizations is determined by means of "tests" completed by managers and employees. These provide readings on (1) Job Maturity (past performance, technical knowledge, understanding of job requirements, problem-solving ability, ability to take responsibility, meeting job experiences, planning skills, decision making skills, follow-through, judgement and problem-identification ability); and (2) Psychological Maturity (willingness to take responsibility, achievement motivation, job commitment, activity level, job interest, persistence, reinforcement required, work attitude, time perspective, supportiveness, initiative, and independence). Most of these dimensions can be applied to the maturity, or level of readiness, in a community as well as to individual members of an organization. In a community, however, these attributes would have to be applied to appropriate community agencies and organizations as well as to individual community members. Relationships within the community would also have to be examined.

It should not be necessary to develop elaborate measuring instruments to assess "task" and and "psychological" factors and then quantify readiness on a numerical scale. A "check list" of factors which can be rated as "low," "moderate," or "high" readiness should be sufficient. The dimensions can be used as a guide in developing such a check list. The following factors should also be considered: (1) the past record of the community in similar activities; (2) the relationships between the community and the school; (3) the relationships within the community; (4) the levels of appropriate skills and motivation within the community; (5) the level of community pride; and (6) the aspirations of the community. Some simple systems for "weighting" these dimensions and arriving at an overall readiness profile must also be developed. The ratings and judgment should be done by a panel of people who are knowledgeable about the community and have the appropriate skills to make the judgments called for.

References

Hersey, P., & Blanchard, K.H. (1977). *Management of organization: behavior: Utilizing human resources.* (3rd ed.). Englewood Cliffs, NJ: Prentice-Hall.

Ingram, E.J., & McIntosh, R.G. (1983). *Education North evaluation projec Final report.* Edmonton: Alberta Education.

Appendix F

A Reporting and Data Collection Model

Education North

Evaluation Project

Report to the Steering Committee

presented by

Ernie Ingram and Gordon McIntosh

March 17, 1980

Department of Educational Administration

University of Alberta

Education North

1. External Evaluation Objectives

I Monitoring
1. To monitor the operations of Education North with respect to its structures, functions, activities, and relationships.
2. To monitor the operations of the local societies established by Education North with respect to their structures, functions, activities, and relationships.

II Evaluating
1. To assess the structures, functions, activities, relationships and outcomes of Education North with respect to the explicit and implicit objectives of the project.
2. To assess the structures, functions, activities, relationships, and outcomes of the projects undertaken by the local societies with respect to the explicit and implicit objectives established for the projects by Education North.
3. To assess the impact of the evaluation activities on the operations and outcomes of the projects of local societies and the overall project.

III Consulting
1. To provide consultative assistance to local societies with respect to the "internal evaluation" of their projects.

IV Reporting
1. To provide information progress reports to each meeting of the Minister's Advisory Committee for Education North.
2. To provide progress reports and to seek advice from the steering committee established for the evaluation project.
3. To provide annual reports and a final report to Alberta Education.
4. To produce a handbook based on the experiences and findings of the project evaluation, and on relevant literature, to assist educators and community development workers in selecting effective ways of working in similar settings.

* * * * * *

3. Data Gathering Activities and Plans

Evaluation Objective I (1)

To monitor the operations of Education North with respect to its structures, functions, activities, and relationships.

Activities

A case description of the development and operation of Education North up to December 31, 1979, has been prepared. Material for the case was obtained from documents from Education North files, interviews with most of the individuals involved in the development and initiation of the projects, and observations of Minister's Advisory Committee meetings.

Plans

1. The continued monitoring of Education North will be done through
   (a) updating the document review on a twice per year basis;
   (b) interviews with involved persons
      – Education North staff (2 or 3 times per year).
      – Minister's Advisory Committee members (once per year).
      – Local society leaders (2 times per year).
      – Other local leaders (once per year).
   (c) A system for keeping a diary of project activities in being considered.
   (d) Observations of MACFEN meetings

Evaluation Objective I(2)

To monitor the operations of the local societies established by Education North with respect to their structures, functions, activities, and relationships.

Activities

A case description of the development and operation of each of the local societies as of December 31, 1979, has been prepared. These include Slave Lake, Fort Vermilion, Little Red River, Lac La Biche, Fort Chipewyan, and Wabasca-Desmarais. Material for the case descriptions was obtained from the documents form Education North and local files, interviews with Education North officers and local people, visits to all local projects except Wabasca-Desmarais, and economic-social-demographic information from a variety of sources.

Plans

1. The continued monitoring of local societies will be done through
    (a) updating the document review on a twice per year basis
    (b) interviews with involved persons
        – Education North staff (2 or 3 times per year)
        – Local society leaders (2 times per year)
        – Other local leaders (once per year)
    (c) the establishment of local "historians" for each society and a system by which these historians can maintain an accurate and in-depth account of the project and the societies' activities.

Evaluation Objective II (1)

To assess the structures, functions, activities, relationships, and outcomes of Education North with respect to the explicit and implicit objectives of the project.

Activities

1. A search of the literature on similar projects is under way.
2. The objectives of Education North have been identified from the documents and interviews.

Plans

1. The list of objectives is to be reviewed and priorized by such groups as the Steering Committee, the evaluation workshop, and the Minister's Advisory Committee.
2. The literature search will be continued.
3. All of the other data necessary will be collected in connection with other objectives.

Evaluation Objective II (2)

To assess the structures, functions, activities, relationships and outcomes of the projects undertaken by the local societies with respect to the explicit and implicit objectives established for the projects by Education North.

Activities

1. The objectives of Education North common to all projects have been identified from documents and interviews.

2. Indicators of achievement or movement toward these objectives have also been identified.
3. Instruments and procedures to collect data on these indicators have been drafted.

Plans

1. The objectives, indicators and instruments will be reviewed at the evaluation workshop.
2. A proposal for co-operative data collection and analysis is being developed and will be presented to the evaluation workshop.
3. If the proposal is approved the system will be put into place.
   - The external evaluators will develop the instruments and procedures in consultation with the Steering Committee and local societies.
   - Local societies will collect the data annually.
   - The external evaluators will analyze the data, make the data available to the appropriate local society, and use the analyses in their reporting.
   - The external evaluators will collect some data themselves through site visits and interviews.
4. Other data needed will be collected in connection with other objectives.

Evaluation Objective II (3)

To assess the impact of the evaluation activities on the operations and outcomes of the projects of local societies and the overall project.

Activities

1. A literature search has been initiated.

Plans

1. The literature search will continue during the next two years.
2. Interviews will be held during each of the three years of the project.

Evaluation Objective III (1)

To provide consultative assistance to local societies with respect to the "internal evaluation" of their projects.

Activities

1. Plans are under way to hold an evaluation workshop, both to collect data relevant to internal evaluations and to start the consultation process.
2. Some data have already been collected about local projects.

Plans

1. Following the evaluation workshop, consultations will be held with local projects.
   – visits (at least 2 times per year)
   – correspondence and telephone consultations
   – other workshops if necessary

Evaluation Objectives IV (1), (2), (3), (4)

1. To provide informal progress reports to each meeting of the Minister's Advisory Committee for Education North.
2. To provide progress reports and seek advice from the Steering Committee established for the Evaluation Project.
3. To provide annual reports and a final report to Alberta Education.
4. To produce a handbook based on the experiences and findings of the project evaluation and relevant literature, to assist educators and community development workers in selecting effective ways of working in similar settings.

Actiivities

1. Informal reports have been made at each Minister's Advisory Committee meeting.
2. A literature review has been initiated.

Plans

1. More formal reports will be made to the Steering Committee. Meetings will be held when appropriate about at least two times per year.
2. Plans have not yet been made for the annual or final reports.
3. The literature review will continue and be intensified in the second year of the project.

The Explicit and Implicit Objectives of Education North

I *Adults*

1. To develop increased parental interest in, support of and participation in educational activities.
2. To enhance the feeling in the community that education is worthwhile.

    – to develop overall community commitment to education activities.

    – to deepen and broaden the base of community support for education.

3. To increase parental influence on the schools.
4. To build and maintain communication links between the school and the community.

    – to lessen the sense of estrangement of community members from the schools

5. To develop community leadership skills.
6. To develop problem solving abilities on the part of community members.
7. To develop community support for teachers.

II *The School*

8. To develop and implement curriculum which is relevant to the community and its members.
9. To develop and implement local curriculum materials.
10. To enhance the involvement of local adults in school programs (curriculum development and instruction).
11. To provide a community-oriented induction process for teachers.

III *Students*

12. To improve students' attitudes to school and society.
13. To increase student involvement in education.
14. To improve student achievement.
15. To nurture personal identity and ambition.

Appendix G

Tables of Contents

PERSONNEL POLICY
AND
CHANGING ENROLLMENT

Commissioned by
EDMONTON CATHOLIC SCHOOL DISTRICT

Mary Abt
Terry Banfield
Gordon Chaytors
Myrna Greene
Robert Henning
Joe Laplante
Frank Letain
Kim Cheng Lim
Cheryl Nattrass
Craig Roxburgh

April 1981
DEPARTMENT OF EDUCATIONAL ADMINISTRATION
THE UNIVERSITY OF ALBERTA • EDMONTON, CANADA

TABLE OF CONTENTS

TOWARDS AN INTERPROVINCIAL COMMUNITY COLLEGE
(Post-secondary Education in East Central Alberta and West Central Saskatchewan)

Commissioned by
Alberta – Advanced Education
Saskatchewan – Department of Continuing Education

Prepared by
Ernest J. Ingram
J. Graham T. Kelsey
Abram G. Konrad
James M. Small

Department of Educational Administration
University of Alberta
July, 1974

TABLE OF CONTENTS

APPENDICES:

TOWARD
A YUKON COLLEGE

(CONTINUING EDUCATION OPPORTUNITIES IN THE YUKON)

Commissioned by
DEPARTMENT OF EDUCATION
GOVERNMENT OF YUKON

Prepared by
Ernest J. Ingram
Abram G. Konrad
James M. Small

DEPARTMENT OF EDUCATIONAL ADMINISTRATION AND
CENTRE FOR THE STUDY OF POSTSECONDARY EDUCATION
UNIVERSITY OF ALBERTA

SEPTEMBER, 1979

TABLE OF CONTENTS

EVALUATING SCHOOL DISTRICTS: A SOURCE BOOK

A Report Prepared for the
Alberta Catholic School Trustees' Association

E.J. Ingram & E. Miklos
Department of Educational Administration
University of Alberta

January, 1980

CONTENTS

Index